Whole Child Reading

A Quick-Start Guide to Teaching Students with
Down Syndrome and Other Developmental Delays

Natalie Hale

Woodbine House

© 2016 Natalie Hale

All rights reserved. Published in the United States of America by
Woodbine House, Inc., 6510 Bells Mill Road, Bethesda, MD 20817.
800-843-7323. www.woodbinehouse.com

Library of Congress Cataloging-in-Publication Data

Names: Hale, Natalie.
Title: Whole child reading : a quick-start guide to teaching students with
  down syndrome and other developmental delays / Natalie Hale.
Description: Bethesda, MD : Woodbine House, 2016. | Includes
bibliographical   references and index.
Identifiers: LCCN 2016033963 (print) | LCCN 2016035748 (ebook) |
ISBN   9781606132838 (pbk.) | ISBN 9781606132845 ()
Subjects: LCSH: Children with mental disabilities--Education. | Reading. |
  Down syndrome. | Developmentally disabled children--Education.
Classification: LCC LC4620 .H35 2016 (print) | LCC LC4620 (ebook) |
DDC
  371.92--dc23
LC record available at https://lccn.loc.gov/2016033963

10 9 8 7 6 5 4 3
Manufactured in the United States of America

CONTENTS

Foreword

As an educator, I collect children's books that teach language concepts, have an early literacy component, and show character diversity. I met Natalie a decade ago at a small conference in southwest Virginia. As I read through her books, I was stunned. She had published a collection of books that met all of my needs, and she was the author and illustrator as well! Every book was appropriate for all children regardless of their abilities. I was truly in awe and knew that she was special.

Now Natalie has called on her knowledge of creating high-interest, effective reading materials to write a book that will help others foster both success and a love of reading in their students. As technology morphs our culture and learning style, information bombards us from all directions. Natalie has filtered and synthesized important teaching concepts that she delivers succinctly in a way that we can clearly understand. This manual meets our needs in teaching literacy to children with developmental disabilities.

Individuals with disabilities have the right to learn to read. As educators, we must presume competence and are obligated to teach reading. Unfortunately, as an educator I too often see my colleagues assuming how much they believe a student will learn, and too often expectations are low, with presumed *in*competence. When I see high school students who are still learning to name letters, it reminds me of Mark Twain's words: "Don't let school get in the way of your education."

Struggling students may not flourish with commercial reading curricula, but that is certainly not a reason to stop teaching literacy. This book provides an option when other programs have failed; significantly, it provides an alternative to commercial curricula and provides the components of a comprehensive literacy program.

These structured shared reading lessons are designed for fluency and comprehension practice, and the flexibility offers room for phonemic awareness through games and phonics instruction. Natalie has also highlighted four important factors to consider when planning instruction and designing specific activities for struggling students: level of intensity, appropriate level of difficulty, motivation, and meaningfulness to the student.

As an educator in public schools (in three different countries), I often read IEPs or learning plans that focus on "reading sight words." Unfortunately, those sight words typically consist of *exit, yield, stop, restroom*, and other functional life-skill words and are taught using flash cards in assessment-type fashion. Slow and boring, and certainly not motivating or engaging! I know firsthand that if you have the child's attention, then you can teach and he or she can learn. Natalie's methodology to "go in through the heart" is a sure way to get the attention of the child and develop a lifelong learner who reads to learn, to discover, and to enjoy.

Natalie did not develop this book while sitting in an office sketching out theories and practices. She synthesized and developed these effective activities and strategies by test-driving them in her work with struggling students with disabilities. She has found success by focusing on students' strengths while improving skills that are weak.

If you are an educator or parent looking for a program to teach reading to anyone who struggles to learn, then you need this book. *Whole Child Reading* is a commonsense approach with easy-to-follow steps that can lead to successful independent reading.

If, as educators and parents, we strive to "presume competence" and guide our struggling learners to confidence and success, this book can be an invaluable tool for us to achieve those goals.

Dr. Jennifer Mitchell, CCC-SLP

CHAPTER 1

Start Here

What Is the Goal of This Book?

This book is designed to be a tool for quick success in the hands of anyone who wants to teach reading to a learner with Down syndrome, autism, or other developmental delays. Brevity is intentionally paramount in this guide; it might just as well have been subtitled *For Educators and Parents with Very Little Time.* You do, in fact, have very little time because of the demands already made on your twenty-four hours.

If you're looking for an exhaustive tome or reference book on teaching reading to children with Down syndrome and other developmental delays, you'll need to read a different book, and I've listed several in the resource list.

But if you're looking for an understanding of how our students can quickly and most easily learn to read and for a condensed view of best practice and materials, then you've got the right book. It is my intention and hope that the small size of this book and the direct style of the writing may serve you well.

My goal is to help you quickly find the information and understanding that you need and then enable you to put this book down and take that information and run with it, regardless of the age or ability of your learner.

Cut to the Chase

Whatever we do in this endeavor of teaching reading, it must be lean and fast. No one has time and energy to waste. Parents are overwhelmed, their time stretched to the limit. Schools are underfunded and teachers are treading water to stay afloat with the demands made on them: with too-large class sizes, with class demographics heavily weighed down by behavioral problems, with barges of paperwork, and with requirements and procedures set by those who don't actually do the teaching.

So let's cut to the chase. Our efforts, our setups in this endeavor, must be streamlined: no extra information, no money spent on materials that aren't going to be effective with our particular students. With this book, you will indeed cut to the chase.

What Is Whole Child Reading?

"We go in through the heart and teach to the brain."

Have you ever tried to teach something difficult to an unwilling student with Down syndrome, autism, or other developmental delays? Of course you have.

As parents and educators, we have all witnessed a student's disappearing act. Children, teens, and adult students are experts at this. We struggle trying to engage students so we can get in the door and help them learn *whatever* it is we're trying to teach them. But if we can't hook the student's interest, that student may shut down, go away, turn off, or otherwise communicate, *"I'm outta here with whatever you're trying to teach me, and I don't care what that is."*

Exactly. We all want to avoid experiencing that, and if we go "in through the heart and teach to the brain," we have the best possible chance of doing just that.

Go in through the Heart...

Very simply, in the beginning of the reading journey, we approach learning *only* through those topics that are nearest and dearest to that student's heart. We put no reading material in front of that student's eyes that does not *directly* focus on those topics. Period. Does this mean you will be creating some homemade personal books in the beginning of the student's journey? And modifying some really cool trade books so your student can read them? Yes. Is that difficult? No. Is it an amazing motivator? Yes.

All other materials and topics can come later, after the learner becomes successful, enthusiastic, and—as a natural result—confident. These three elements—success, enthusiasm, and confidence—develop together and form an unbeatable impetus toward more advanced reading ability.

And Teach to the Brain

While we're using the motivational key that opens the door—going in through the heart—it's crucial that we use teaching materials that are designed for easy access and rapid assimilation and retention by the brain. This means using a special high-focus format, the Fast Flash method, "Sandwich Style Teaching," and more. We need to understand *what* the brain sees and *how* the brain sees and retains what it does and then capitalize on that. We want to make it easy for the brain; knowing how to do this is one of the core focuses of this book.

Literacy Is the New Norm

Illiteracy is no longer a viable option for individuals with Down syndrome, autism, and other developmental delays. In the United States, literacy is fast becoming the expectation and the norm for our children, largely due to the accumulation of new data concerning best practice, and the promotion of that knowledge by parents and support organizations, some of which specifically target getting this information into school systems.

But even at this writing, many school systems and educators are not yet equipped with that knowledge and training. This is not the fault of either educators or parents; that information was not part of their own curriculum or knowledge pool until now.

It's my hope that this guide can support the turning of that tide in the direction of literacy for learners with delays.

But What Are *Your* Goals?

I've given you the goal of this book; but let's look at *your* goal in teaching reading to your child or student, and let's look at your time and dollar restrictions in getting there.

For all readers of this book, the goal is, of course, lifelong literacy for our learners, with its immediate impact of inclusion in classroom reading and writing activities. The student can participate with his peers and is not left literarily languishing on the sidelines, bored and probably acting out.

For the child in school, learning to read at the early age of four or five can also make a massive difference in his educational experience. A great deal of research done by Down Syndrome Education International in the United Kingdom has shown that early literacy support has an exponentially positive effect on the *entire* academic years of a child. The earlier a child learns to read, the greater his success in school all the way through high school. The effect is permanent and long-lasting; we couldn't ask for better results.

If you are a parent, reaching this goal offers your child the gift of a lifetime: inclusion in the world of print, the world of information and entertainment. No doors are closed to your child…he can simply *read*. No exclusion is possible; no one can prevent him from absorbing the necessary, instructive, or entertaining information surrounding him. This is inclusion-versus-exclusion at its most communicative level. As parents, the moment when we first witness our child reading independently is one we never forget.

Where Does This Information Come From?

Like mighty tributaries flowing into one river, there are many sources for the information I give you in this book. They include the decades of research and teaching done by Down Syndrome Education International in the United Kingdom, the seminal literacy work of Dr. Glenn Doman and his pediatric colleagues at the Institutes for the Achievement of Human Potential (IAHP), the extraordinarily successful work of his nephew Robert Doman and the National Association for Child Development (NACD), new research in the relatively new field of the neurology of learning around the world, the seminal work of Patricia Oelwein at the University of Washington, the legacy of Maria Montessori, and the work of "Right Brain Education" Japanese educator Makoto Shichida.

Added to that are the methods I've developed in teaching children with Down syndrome as well as children with a dual diagnosis of Down syndrome and autism spectrum disorder (DS/ASD), along with information from the networking that accumulates with twenty-six years of teaching reading work-shops around the country and across borders.

How to Use This Book

The chapters are arranged to give information in the order in which you will most likely need it, detailing the whys and hows of teaching reading quickly (yes, quickly) to learners with developmental delays by going in through the heart and teaching to the brain.

The final chapter outlines a simple scaffold for teaching reading, from the first steps of reading aloud to an infant through sight word reading (logographic reading), phonics (alphabetic reading), and all the way to skilled independent reading (orthographic reading.)

If your learner is already somewhere in the middle of that reading spectrum (logographic-alphabetic-orthographic), you may be tempted to skip the instructions and jump in at the most relevant point. But since best practice for teaching reading successfully to children with developmental delays is not yet well known, I encourage you to read through the book in the order given. This will avoid missed steps and consequent backpedaling, which is much more labor-intensive than cruising ahead full speed!

Terminology: I use the words *child, student,* and *learner* interchangeably and alternate genders by chapter when referring to learners with Down syndrome and other disabilities: male in odd numbered chapters, female in even chapters. But this is not a book about teaching children only: *best practice is the same for our teens and adults* with special needs who are not yet fluent readers. Most readers of this book are working with children, so in most cases it will be an apt term, but I intend those terms to refer to all learners.

It's Always Too Early to Say, "It Can't Be Done"

An aerospace engineer friend of mine is fond of joking, even at the last minute before hitting an impossible deadline, "It's *still* too early to panic." Echoing that spirit, it is my firm belief that it is *never too late* for a learner with special needs to progress in reading. At the very least we want to help him to the point where reading ability can be relied on in daily life, and at the very best we want him to reach the point of fully independent, fluent reading. We want to give him the gift of being able to read both for information and for the pure joy of diving headlong into the magic other-worlds offered by literacy.

You Have Only Two Options

Two Choices

You have only two choices when approaching teaching reading to learners with special needs. One works and the other doesn't.

Start and Stop

Option 1 is very common and guarantees frustration for students, parents, and educators. I see this situation most often when desperate parents bring me their teenagers who can't read. The teens missed the boat somehow, and parents want to grab one last chance to make it happen.

A typical description of Option 1 is as follows: Megan starts off in kindergarten with a terrific teacher who launches her on the reading path. Megan is excited, and so are her parents. All goes well for a year or two—she's really catching on! Then Megan moves on into another classroom where the teacher doesn't have the same knowledge or insight. Megan's parents don't realize this yet and trust that Megan's reading will continue to progress. Preoccupied with the needs of their other children and with Megan's various therapies, Mom and Dad forget about reading for a while until they realize that Megan has forgotten nearly all the words she used to know and that reading progress has gone into reverse drive.

Conferring with the teacher doesn't help, because the teacher hasn't been trained in the specific approaches Megan needs, so Mom or Dad buckle down at home and manage for a while to teach Megan themselves. But Megan's parents are overwhelmed and unsure how to go about it, so success and enthusiasm wane after a while.

The ball gets bounced back and forth with a start-and-stop motion, and by the time she's a teen, poor Megan is frustrated and convinced she can never learn to read. She acts out, objects to every attempt to be taught reading, and effectively blocks the possibility of learning; she's afraid to fail again.

Pedal to the Metal

Option 2 works; it requires a commitment to frequency, and the reward is that *you will work yourself out of a job*. Once you have taught your learner to read, you will never, ever have to teach her to read again. It's a done deal. When reading is taught consistently, without lapses of time, it becomes the permanent possession of the reader. Once an orthographic (independent, automatic) reader, always an orthographic reader. You and I don't need to think about reading when we do it—it's automatic, effortless. When we launch a child as an enthusiastic, independent reader, our job is done.

Does that mean that the student will hunker down with novels for the rest of her life? Maybe, maybe not. As an adult, she may gravitate toward smaller books or magazines—and certainly electronic tablets or any screens that will transport her to the Internet. Everyone has different interests and preferences, and hers will lead her to her reading material of choice.

What does this option require? Here's my Reading Rx: *five minutes twice a day.* Six out of seven days if possible. This is where we start, and as success and its naturally accompanying enthusiasm build, so does the time invested in learning. Five minutes becomes ten, becomes fifteen, becomes twenty...

The teacher intuitively gauges when to extend reading time and ideally stops just before the student actually wants to. We want to leave her wanting more. This time extension will happen naturally and painlessly if we "go in through the heart and teach to the brain."

What Can I Possibly Get Done in Five Minutes?

You'll see! Keep reading and I'll give you a plan. We'll start simply with a super-high-interest personal book and its accompanying flash cards (which will be taught with the Fast Flash method) and we'll sandwich reading the book in between two quick sessions of teaching the words. And that's just the beginning.

Your Decision

Choosing either Option 1 or 2 is your decision, but it's the moment of truth: only repetition and frequency will get the job done. In the beginning of the learning process, what our children knew on Monday, they don't know on Wednesday. This is normal, and we actually expect that to happen with children with developmental delays. Information will float in and out of retention until it's permanent. Repetition and frequency make permanence happen—along with the essential "heart and brain" elements explained in this book.

If you've chosen the "pedal to the metal" approach—which I'm sure you have if you've still got this book open—then your next question might be, "How in the world am I going to fit this into my schedule?" Good question, and I suggest coming up with Plans A, B, and C for a good time to teach. Teachers are better equipped to fit *Whole Child Reading* into their already-structured teaching day, but parents will need Plan A and one or two back-up plans in the event the first plan fails. If parents have thought through only one teaching-time possibility and it doesn't work out, it will be tempting to throw in the towel. Wisdom inclines us to have a backup plan or two.

Ideally, parents will want to pick a time that not only works for the whole family but fits these requirements: a time when the child is not hungry, tired, or in a bad mood—and when the parent is not hungry, tired, or in a bad mood!

So assuming you've chosen Option 2, here we go...

CHAPTER 3

A Few Short Truths

Adopt and Hold on to a Few Short Truths

In addition to the wisdom, "Go in through the heart and teach to the brain," there are a few basic tenets that we need to embrace and act on. Here they are:

It's Never Too Late

It is never, ever too late for someone with developmental delays to begin learning to read. My oldest student came to me at age thirty-three; he had Down syndrome and was legally blind. With his triple challenge of age, Down syndrome, and seriously compromised vision, I had to get quite creative with my teaching, but we worked it out with the help of a gigantic white board and the USC Trojans (his top interest in life; more about that later when we talk about motivation). The day that he read one of my *Special Reads* pre-primer reading books aloud to his little nieces and nephews, his mom cried. She'd never thought she would see that happen.

Sue Buckley, director of research and training at the Down Syndrome Education International (UK), mirrors my own experience with her comment in *Reading and Writing Development for Teenagers with Down Syndrome:* "It is always too early to say that children, young people, or adults cannot learn to read…Children with Down syndrome can 'take off' with reading at any age." Sometimes it's the teenagers with delays who surprise us with a sudden interest in learning to read; peer pressure has its benefits! Buckley adds, Buckley adds in the same *iiSeries* in the volume for *Teenagers with Down syndrome, 11-16 years:* "Data…indicates that we should expect significant progress in literacy skills during the teen-age years for most pupils. There is no evidence that a learning 'plateau' has been reached or that it is too late to begin reading instruction." (See the References at the back of the book for this valuable resource.)

If we can ignite the interest of teens or adults and give them materials with which they *can* succeed, we've got a good chance of making it happen for them.

Being Nonverbal Is No Impediment to Reading

I wish I could say this a thousand times to encourage both parents and educators: *being nonverbal is no impediment to learning to read.* The truth is that some of my best little readers are completely nonverbal, on the severe end of the CAS scale (childhood apraxia of speech). I taught them the same way I taught the rest of my students, but of course I tested them differently.

The plight of children with developmental delays who are mentally bright as the sun but also nonverbal (or nearly so) touches me most, because the worst is assumed in school: "if he can't talk, there must not be much going on inside." The opposite can be true: if a very bright mind is locked in silence, the child is probably acting out in frustration.

For children who are somewhere in the middle or mild end of that nonverbal spectrum, the extremely good news is that teaching reading is one of the most effective ways to teach talking. This is backed up by evidence-based practice done over the last thirty years by Down Syndrome Education International. For many of these children, when they read aloud it is the first time in their lives that they have strung three, five, or more words together. As reading progresses, this transfers over into speech patterns, and the result is thrilling.

Task Size

Task size must be manageable. "Manageable" in this case means designed for success. It must be within the student's capability. If the learner says or communicates, "It's too hard," then guess what? *It's too hard.* There are other ways our students tell us a task is beyond them: they turn away, shut down, act out…they get creative in their objections. It simply means that the task we've put in front of them is more than they can handle, and they are afraid they'll fail. So reduce the task size until it matches their capability. Correct task size = success, self-esteem, and confidence.

This guideline of ensuring appropriate task size is vital in teaching children with special needs, and it applies to anything and everything we will ever teach them.

Frequency

I've already mentioned the importance of frequency; let's talk about the *why* of that advice. Why is frequency so important for students with Down syndrome and other developmental disabilities? Let's look at the brain for a minute.

Very simply stated, every time a bit of information is processed by the brain, it sparks connections between the neurons. These messages must travel along the myelin sheath, the plasma membrane wrapped around nerve axons. Myelin is both an electrical insulator *and* a conductor, and every time that same information is transmitted along the neural pathway, the myelin sheath thickens. This happens with lightening speed, and eventually has the effect of making that information easy to access. With enough repetitions, it becomes permanent—like remembering how to walk or run. The more repetitions that travel that neural highway, making connections and firing synapses, the thicker the myelin sheath gets and the more easily that information is transported. We want thicker myelin sheaths for our readers! And it only gets that way through repetition.

This is why, when we teach sight words with the Fast Flash method, we show the words repeatedly—and rapidly—as you'll see when we talk about Fast Flash in chapter 8.

Duration

What is the appropriate *duration* of a teaching unit when working with a student? As long as it takes, and probably longer than you thought. In other words, whatever the timeframe turns out to be for a teaching unit, that's the right duration. You might expect a task to be learned in, say, two months. In fact, it may take four. Expect this and factor the extra time into your teaching plan. Mastering a task will take longer than it would for neurotypical learners; that's expected, and that's fine.

CHAPTER 4

Personal Books: The Magic Door

This Is How We "Go in through the Heart"

If you take away nothing else from this book except the habit of creating personal books and you apply it continuously and *progressively*, your work will be half done. Personal books are major motivators and open the door to enthusiasm and keen attention. In terms of the neurology of teaching, personal books are the perfect tool: engaging, motivating, fun, and interactive with the child's life, each book a new experience. It brings the learner on board. For that reason, if for no other, personal books come first.

The Eleventh Commandment

Some years ago I wrote an eleventh commandment (cheeky, I know). I show it in all my workshops, and it goes like this:

*"Thou shalt not dare to teach children with special needs anything that interests them not; verily, they shall be interested **only** in what they are interested in, and shall*

not *be interested in any other thing. Woe unto those who do not revere and abide by this commandment! Amen."*

Personal books are your opportunity to obey that eleventh commandment!

Go in through the Heart...

If someone is sleeping and we want to tell her something very important, we wake her up first. Personal books are the wake-up call for students with Down syndrome and other developmental disabilities—*regardless of age, ability, or interests.* I cannot think of any reason why there would be an exception to this.

Every individual is looking at the world from the inside out; they themselves are *home.* And home, where the heart is, is of highest interest to them. This is supremely true for learners with developmental delays. They understand home. So to capture their "awakeness"—their readiness to learn—and to get those neuromodulators pumping, as I'll describe in later chapters, we go in through the heart with what matters most. Personal books get that job done.

So What Are Personal Books?

Personal books are homemade reading books written about a learner's absolutely favorite things in life. You create them yourself, along with flash cards for all words not yet mastered by the child.

Topics can include virtually anything that the person loves: people, pets, sports, TV characters, favorite music, and, of course, food. Through personal books, we can turn anything around to *reading.* For example, if a child is addicted to using her iPad, we can create a personal reading book about how she loves her iPad. Almost no topic is forbidden; we use every avenue we can to get inroads to that "awakeness" state so we can teach. In addition to delighting and motivating the learner by giving her a chance to read about herself and the things she loves, personal books can be healing.

My son Jonathan has Down syndrome, attention deficit hyperactivity disorder (ADHD), and oppositional defiant disorder (ODD). I began creating personal reading books for him when he was five; he loved them, could read them, and carried them everywhere. One unfortunate day when Jonathan was in first grade, a classmate closed a steel door on his little finger. The resulting trauma involved a trip to the hospital, the experience of being strapped (trapped) in a "papoose" so the doctor could stitch up the finger without using general anesthesia…you get the idea.

A friend who is a speech/language pathologist suggested that, while I was making so many personal books, why not do one about this trauma? I recoiled at the idea initially, but later I thought better of it and took her suggestion, ending the book with—of course—"My little finger is all better now. See?" The effect that this book had on Jonathan was amazing: for a full six months, his *My Little Finger* book was his number-one book preference; it went everywhere with him. After about six months, he quietly put it aside and only occasionally took it out after that. I was stunned when I realized that this simple personal book had enabled him to *process the trauma*. It was truly over for him.

What Are Social Stories?

I use the lowercased term "social stories" in this book to refer to personal books all grown up—to personal books that are written for specific practical purposes rather than to delight the reader. (I am using the term as special educators commonly do today to denote personal stories that are used as facilitators and way-smoothers. I am not talking about the "Social Stories" first developed in 1990 by Carol Gray in her work with children with autism, nor am I referring specifically to Gray's design and methods.)

Social stories help our learners adjust to transitions, new experiences, difficulties in life, routine schedules, doctor and dentist visits—you name it. They can even help heal where there is a trauma, a loved one's death, the temporary absence of a parent, a transition to a new school, etc. There is no limit to the use we can make of social stories throughout the individual's entire life.

Two examples: when my son was thirteen, it was no longer appropriate for either Mom or Dad to help him bathe properly. Problem: his idea of taking a bath was to fill the tub, sit in it for two seconds, get out, and towel dry. Enter a nifty social story book: we took pictures of each step along the bath routine, from using the toilet beforehand to finally turning off the light. We interjected pictures from one of his favorite movies, and peppered it with goofy phrases that he and his dad loved to laugh over. We laminated the entire book to make it waterproof and bound it, and that became his bath instructor. Problem solved!

Much later, after high school graduation, Jonathan was enrolled in a transition program on a university campus. Even at that age, he still struggled with the impulsivity component of his second-of-three diagnoses, severe ADHD. That made it difficult for him to stick to his independent schedule on campus. So if he was struck with the inspiration to go exploring rather than keeping to his duties, he did just that. He went exploring. With his innately excellent sense of direction (if I take a wrong turn in the car, he yells, "Wrong way!"), getting lost was not a problem. But going off task was a definite problem. So the staff created a social story about his daily routine, and he had to begin each day of training with a mandatory reading of that book. It worked.

Essential Design Plan for Personal Books

I recommend a very specific design for personal books. Why be so persnickety? Because of the brain's preferences and abilities. I want to get in the door as quickly as possible to help the reader progress; to do that, I have to deliberately design my format to be very brain-friendly. If you follow my lead, you will not only create a fantastically interesting (to the learner) reading book, but an extremely useful teaching tool that can later be used as a testing tool. That's because students see no pictures for reference (until a page turn later), so you'll know whether she's actually reading or not.

Here are the *essential design elements* of effective personal books:

1. The topic is of very high interest to the learner.

2. The on-topic pictures involve the learner (eating, playing, etc., according to the specific topic chosen).

3. Type size is large, between 32 point and 130 point, depending on the learner's reading level.

4. The font used is always a sans serif font (see below).

5. Double or even triple spacing is used between each word.

6. Extra spacing ("leading," pronounced "ledding") is used between lines of type.

7. Left-hand pages are left blank (good use of white space) for the emergent reader.

8. Text stands alone on the right-hand page for the emergent reader.

9. That same text is repeated on the following right-hand page, with a picture above the text.

10. Page setup is "landscape" (horizontal) format to allow space for larger font use.

11. The final right-hand page says "The End" because of the psychological boost it gives the child: "I just read a whole book!"

Sample Pages

Shown below are sample pages of a personal book created for an emergent reader. And who is an emergent reader? Simply put, a learner who is at the beginning of the literacy adventure—interested in books, beginning to learn letter sounds and images, learning to follow the words on a page, and knowing the names of things. Phonological as well as phonemic awareness is only beginning at this emergent point, and the reader has mastered fewer than forty sight words. In other words, at this level the learner is just starting to acquire the skills of identifying individual sounds (phonemes) and being able to manipulate the many units of oral language.

Note that as specified in point 7 above, I recommend not using the left-hand pages in books for emergent readers. Leaving the left pages as blank white space tells the brain exactly where to look: "Look elsewhere!" In this illustration of pages 1 and 2, white space tells the brain to look at the text. In pages 3 and 4, the brain will look first at the picture and then secondarily drop down and give a cursory look at the line of type. We don't mind that disproportionate focus time because on page 2, we've already given the brain a full dose of the text without any competition.

This example shows pages approximately 11" wide by 8.5" high; you are seeing two pages open together (a "double spread"). Type size is approximately 1 inch high, or 130 points in the Tahoma font.

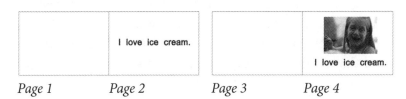

Page 1   Page 2   Page 3   Page 4

To repeat: notice also that the pages are designed in a landscape format, not portrait format. This is essential in the beginning stages, since the landscape format gives us more width for the text line; more page width allows us to use a larger font size.

Why No Pictures on the First Page of Type?

Why can't we show pictures along with text on all the pages of our personal books? Doesn't the picture make it easier for the child to learn to read, by reference?

No.

It doesn't help, and in most cases, it hinders. *As the reader progresses*, we can use pictures on the same visual plane. But before the child reaches some fluency and skill, that often delays rather than aids progress. Why? The strongest reason is one I've mentioned before: the brain's attention is grabbed by the picture. The picture holds on tight to that attention, and it is difficult to switch attention to the boring black squiggly lines accompanying the picture, which at the moment are meaningless to the learner.

To quote from DSEI's *Reading and Writing Development* series again, "[Students] learn to read words faster if words are *not* attached to pictures."

The second reason we don't want to include pictures with the type in the early stages is that inexperienced readers, wanting to be successful, will look to the picture for a cue. Using pictures for reference can be helpful only in more experienced stages of reading. For an emergent reader, it causes a train wreck 90 percent of the time, with the reader substituting a word that might (or might not) be related to the picture but bears no resemblance to the actual word she is supposed to be reading. Phonemic awareness goes out the window; she's faking it, and once that "pretend reading" habit gets ingrained, it's very hard to break. This is particularly true of our learners who long to please parents and teachers and don't want to appear to fail. In their view, *any* word is better than no word, and that's how that bad habit is born.

So when a child is in the earliest stages of learning to read, the picture follows a page turn. In that position, it's a visual and emotional reward; it's not visual competition. I recommend repeating the text *on the second page along with the picture.* That's fine, and doesn't distract, because we've already given the brain a "text alone" page. So each line of our text is going to be repeated (once alone, once with a picture). The second time the brain sees it, the "rewarding" picture accompanies it.

Let's Make a Book

Here are the steps for creating personal books, from start to finish. To brainstorm ideas for your learner, you'll need pencil and paper. You'll be writing down your choices associated with each step.

1. **Choose three categories.** From the suggestions below, make a list of three topics of *top interest* for the learner. Having a cache of three topics will give you a great springboard for future personal books, so you won't need to revisit this list later.

   a. Family and friends
   b. Pets
   c. Food
   d. Restaurants
   e. Sports
   f. Music
   g. Movies
   h. TV shows
   i. Other activities, things

2. **Choose one topic.** For now, choose one of those topics.

3. **Decide on a specific title within that topic.** Go from the general to the specific at this point. For instance, you don't want to write "Movies" as a book title; you want to build a book around a favorite movie. So you need to choose a specific title, such as *Frozen, Minions,* etc.

4. **Choose five to seven high-interest words associated with that particular topic.** Taking the movie *Frozen* as an example, your high interest words might be *Elsa, Anna, magic, Olaf, fun, sisters,* and *Frozen.*

5. **Look at a high-frequency word list (e.g., Dolch or Fry) and find your learner's level.** These lists are available as free downloads from many places on the Internet; one good site is www.mrsperkins.com. Mrs. Perkins offers free Dolch word lists from pre-primer through third grade, downloadable as either Word

documents or PDFs. For the Fry Word List, go to www. k12reader.com and type "Fry Words" in the search box. As you take a look at these lists, *find the level that your learner has not fully mastered.* You'll want to focus on this list if possible, as these lists were compiled in order of words most frequently read in common language use. So we naturally want our students to master the most frequently used words first; less pain, more gain.

6. **Choose seven to nine high-frequency words that might work well with your selected high-interest word list.** Continuing with the *Frozen* example, we might choose these high frequency words: *is, love, are, play, and, make, have, I, with.*

7. **STOP. Write down the age and reading level of the learner. Don't go any further until you've done this.** In my reading workshops, attendees waste workshop time when they forge ahead without figuring this out first. Why is it so important?

   a. **Age:** the book you're going to create has to be age appropriate. What's going to be perfect for a six-year-old emergent reader won't work for a twenty-eight-year-old emergent reader. Set the age first in your mind.

   b. **Reading level:** the current reading ability of the student is going to determine the vocabulary list, the number of words in a sentence, the number of sentences on a page, and general complexity. For a five-year-old emergent reader, "I love Mommy" might be a perfect sentence, and the only text on the entire page. For a football-crazy teen or young adult reading at a first-grade level, "The San Francisco 49-ers is my favorite football team. I like to watch their games on TV" might be perfect for one page of type.

One size does not fit all. You don't want to spend precious time doing work that you later have to discard because it didn't fit both age and reading ability, so stop here and *get these two critical bits of information down on paper: age of the learner and current reading level.*

8. **Based on that age and level, decide the format specifics.** Decide how long your sentences should be, how large the type should be, how much text you should put on a page, and the number of pages the book should ideally have. Some examples are provided below as a general guideline. *Please feel free to be flexible within those guidelines once you've got the knack of creating personal books:*

   a. **Emergent reading level** (see definition of emergent reader on page 22 of this chapter): three-or-four-word sentences, one sentence to a page, 130 point type. Six or seven sentences total for a book is ideal for this level. Since each page will have only one sentence, and that same sentence will be repeated on the following page *with* a picture, a six-sentence book will have twelve pages total when it's finished.

   b. **Pre-primer or primer reading level** (the reader is in the process of mastering the first two Dolch word lists or the first Fry list along with many content words): five- to six-word sentences, one or two sentences to a page, 72 point type. Six or seven pages total is also ideal for this level. Since each page will have only one or two sentences, and those same sentences will be repeated on the following page *with* a picture, a six-page book will be a twelve-page book when it's finished.

c. **First-grade reading level** (the reader is in the process of mastering the first grade Dolch list or the second Fry word list, gaining fluency and speed): longer sentences, several sentences to a page, 24- to 32-point type. At this point, I suggest *not* duplicating each page as in (a) and (b) examples. Rather, the first right-hand page contains a several-sentence paragraph; the second right-hand page does not contain any type, but simply shows an illustration/picture as the reading "reward." We are asking more of the reader at this point, so it's helpful to give her a bigger reward at that page turn: big picture, no text.

To clarify: at this level, a page of text (paragraph) is followed by a page with only a picture, and that pattern is repeated through the end of the book. Effort-relax-effort-relax is the system used here, and it works well to give the brain some "break time."

9. **Stick to that format! Don't vary it. *Be consistent.*** One common mistake I see is mixing up the format, abandoning the "age + reading level" formula you've already taken the time to think through. Here's an example of what *not* to do:

a. First text page: "My dog Ruby is brown."

b. Second text page: "Ruby is a cocker spaniel. I really like cocker spaniels because they are cute and friendly and like to play."

c. *No.* This mixes levels and wrecks the usefulness and appropriateness of the book. It won't be comfortable for the reader to master, and would discourage rather than encourage success.

10. **Write the book—finally!** You can finally now get down to the creative part. Within the format guidelines you picked, write the sentences that will comprise the text of the book. How many pages and sentences? That depends on what you wrote down in your notes as an answer to number 8. Stick with that formula.

11. **Sample book:** Continuing with the *Frozen* example, if you were writing a personal book for an eight-year old girl who is an emergent reader and just beginning to learn the pre-primer high frequency list, you might write the book as follows, with *all pages being the right-hand pages in the book,* and therefore listed as "odd" page numbers (even page numbers are the left-hand blank pages). Notice the double spacing between words!

   a. Page 1: I love Frozen.
   b. Page 3: I love Frozen. (with a picture above the text)
   c. Page 5: Frozen is fun.
   d. Page 7: Frozen is fun. (with a picture)
   e. Page 9: Anna and Elsa are sisters.
   f. Page 11: Anna and Elsa are sisters. (with a picture)
   g. Page 13: Elsa makes frozen magic.
   h. Page 15: Elsa makes frozen magic. (with a picture)
   i. Page 17: Elsa makes Olaf.
   j. Page 19: Elsa makes Olaf. (with a picture)
   k. Page 21: Anna plays with Olaf.
   l. Page 23: Anna plays with Olaf. (with a picture)
   m. Page 25: Anna and Olaf and Elsa have fun.

n. Page 27: Anna and Olaf and Elsa have fun. (with a picture)

o. Page 29: I love Frozen.

p. Page 31: I love Frozen.

q. Page 33: The End

12. **Adding pictures:** You have two basic resources for adding pictures: downloading photos from the Internet and taking pictures with your smart phone/camera. You will, of course, need to take some pictures yourself, since each personal book you create is, by definition, personal to the child. Pictures of "me!" are the best motivators.

13. **Print the Book.** Print the book on a computer (not handwritten) and follow the guidelines for page layout: use landscape format, with the font size and sentences you've already made note of on your list. Don't forget to double or triple space between words! It makes a big difference for ease of learning to read. Don't use a bold font; it makes the words harder to read. Though that sounds counterintuitive, it's the truth. Don't use bold.

14. **Laminate. Or not.** Whether you laminate pages before binding or not depends on the age and personality of the student. Your decision. If you know in advance that paper will be tattered into oblivion, go for lamination so your labor of love lasts forever. An alternative is to put each page in a plastic sleeve protector (see the next point about binding).

15. **Bind the book.** I recommend getting plastic coil binding at an office supply store because it lasts and is easier for page-turning. If you take a second to crimp the ends of the plastic coil even more than the office store

did, it will never unravel. Other options for making a book are a) three-hole punching and then using rings to keep the pages together or putting them in a three-ring binder; b) using plastic portfolios (with top-loading plastic sleeves); c) using whatever else you can think of. But I recommend coil binding because it creates the impression of a "real book." With the amount of effort that it takes to create personal books, I think they deserve the very few dollars it takes to bind them.

16. **Teach "sandwich style" and test with errorless testing techniques.** (See chapters 8 and 9 on those two topics.)

Make Flash Cards for the Words

You'll want to make flash cards for all the words in the personal book that the student has not yet mastered. In the case of the *Frozen* example, you'd need to make sixteen flash cards for the sixteen words in the book.

Guidelines for making the cards:

1. **Make the cards large.** The ideal type size is one-inch high for general purposes. For toddlers or preschoolers, two-inch high type is best. (See Glenn Doman's book *How to Teach Your Baby to Read* for guidelines for the youngest emergent readers.)

2. **Type the cards** on a computer; don't try to do handwritten versions if possible. If you need to freehand the cards, draw pencil guidelines first so your letters will all be the same height, and the child's brain won't have extra work to do trying to decipher your writing. Whether you're using a computer or attempting freehand with a marker and carefully drawn guidelines, choose red for the font color. While we use a black font

to create text in our books (modeling every book the learner will ever read in the future), we use red for the flash cards because the brain finds that attractive for learning (more on that in the next chapter.)

3. Set your Word document **"page setup"** for flash cards in one of two ways:

   a. Landscape orientation for printing "2-up" flash cards on standard size paper, 8.5" x 11". Print on cardstock-weight paper, 100 or 110 pounds, available at any office store. Cut each sheet in half lengthwise when printing is finished.

   b. Portrait orientation for printing on blank 5" x 8" index cards.

4. Handwrite your word cue on the back of the card; no one but you will see this, so you don't need to bother with printing it through a computer. Too much trouble.

Here are visual cues for these two setup plans:

   a. Print landscape page setup on 8.5" x 11" index stock and cut the sheet in half lengthwise (below).

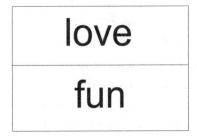

   OR

b. Print portrait page setup for 5" x 8" blank index cards and adjust your paper feeder to fit the stack of cards (below).

c. If you're not on friendly terms with your computer's printer, you could print the words on regular bond paper and cut and paste them onto 5" x 8" index cards, though that can get awkward when it comes to flashing the cards quickly.

d. If you don't have a computer, and you're a professional calligrapher, then by all means go for hand-made! But if you're not a professional and really need to create these cards by hand, make yourself a guide and draw pencil lines on each card before you use a red marker to write the word. That will at least ensure that the letters are all the same size. When I created my son's first flash cards, dinosaurs still roamed the hills, and we did not have a computer. Among other professions, I *was* a calligrapher and drew those pencil lines as a guide anyway!

Can I Create Personal Books Using All Caps?

Some teachers use all capital letters when teaching reading. Should you create personal books using all caps for consistency?

No. Never. Everything we do should make sense and be forward-thinking. We plan for the future: *every book your child will ever read will be printed with text in "sentence case,"* meaning in lowercase letters except for the first letters in proper names and the first letters of sentences. We create personal books modeled on normal reading patterns, not a temporary teaching tool that might be used in the classroom.

Can I Use Apps to Create Personal Books?

Yes, if you first make sure that you can *print* the books from the device. Many children with Down syndrome, autism, or other disabilities spend far too much time with devices as it is, and a book in hand is what we're after. Researchers concerned with the efficacy of "screen learning" have done studies that show print-in-hand learning as significantly more effective for the brain than on-screen-learning. That said, here are some apps that might be useful, but first do some research to determine if you can actually print from these free apps: *Story Creator, Little Story Maker, Picturebook, Story Me,* and *Kid in Story Reader.*

On the computer, it's a snap to use Microsoft Office's PowerPoint software to create personal books. The software is very easy to use, and, of course, printing is no problem.

And Can I Use Apps to Create Flash Cards?

Yes, though it's not optimal from a brain-friendly point of view, you can. Here is a free app that has some useful teaching options: *Sight Words.* You can set the speed of the flash cards (I recommend the fastest setting, one word per 0.7 second). You can also create your own groups of words, turn the sound on or off, and change the font and font size. (I recommend the largest font size.)

National Treasures!

The books you create this way are very nearly national treasures; certainly they will be treasured by your budding reader. Since they are so intrinsic to the very heart and life of the learner, their appeal lasts much longer than the years it takes to learn to read fluently. My thirty-one-year old son astonished me recently by asking if I still had the zoo book I had made for him based on his sixth-grade trip to the zoo! He *remembered* it. You can look forward to the same book affection from your own child. It's remarkable.

CHAPTER 5

Designing for the Brain

Helping the Brain

In order to "teach to the brain," we need to first *design* for the brain. Building on the early literacy-centered work of Glenn Doman and his colleagues at the Institutes for the Achievement of Human Potential (IAHP), we can design *all* reading materials in a brain-friendly format. That is the second and vital half of the equation of "we go in through the heart and teach to the brain." It does little good if we go to the trouble of targeting a child's specific high interests but then design materials that his brain has to struggle to grasp, much less retain.

Our target goal is to make reading as easy as possible for the brain, and there are specific elements that are essential for this to happen. Though the rules are few, they're not optional.

Size, in Fact, Matters

One of the earliest discoveries made at the IAHP was that, across the board, the font size used in teaching reading is *too small*. Using very large type transforms the learning experience. You can almost hear the brain shouting, "I CAN SEE THAT!"

I'll quote from a letter I received from Greg Czarnecki, the educator and parent who trained for years at the IAHP and who first cracked open that magic reading door for my child by opening my own eyes. "For those with handicaps, we make reading impossible by forcing miniature abstract words into their sight," he wrote. "I don't know a single two-year-old who doesn't know that the giant yellow lighted M on the side of the road stands for McDonald's fast food. Make letters large enough and attach to them something known, and children, no matter how low in IQ, will intuit meaning."

Doman's book *How to Teach Your Baby to Read* has been in print for over fifty years and has been translated into more than a dozen languages. Why? Because it works. And the method begins with flash cards boasting two-inch-high red letters. There are researched brain reasons for the red color (humans, even adult humans, are attracted to red, given a preference), and brain reasons for the height. About the height: we're dealing with underdeveloped or immature visual pathways when we're teaching emergent readers; age really doesn't matter. Immaturity of the visual pathway does. A thirty-year-old who can't read still has an underdeveloped visual pathway. The brain's ability to recognize and process tiny black squiggles is quite sophisticated, but that ability develops gradually.

If you still doubt the brain's need for oversized type in the beginning, try this test. Offer your learner two different versions of the material you're trying to teach: one at a large font size (32 to 110 point) and one at a standard classroom font size (somewhere between 12 and 18, depending on the age of the students). Ask your learner which one he wants to read. Hands down, he will pick the larger font. Why? *Because it's easier to read.*

In *How to Teach Your Baby to Read,* Doman devotes most of a page to this one sentence: "The trouble is that we have made the print too small." The sentence is repeated several times, each time at a smaller type size, going all the way down to 6 point. He gets his "point" across. The brain struggles to read small type.

A quarter of a century ago when I began to create my son's personal books, I misunderstood something that may account for the astonishing speed at which my five-year-old with an average-IQ-for-Down-syndrome learned to read independently. My misunderstanding? I thought that the *books* I created had to have two-inch high type as well as the flash cards. So his first book did. The book had no pictures whatsoever until the last triumphant page, and it took him only two weeks to learn to read it and master the eleven vocabulary words it contained.

Continuing in my fortuitous ignorance, the next books I created had type over an inch high. As you can imagine, these books were monstrous in size, created on poster board twenty-four or more inches wide. I very gradually reduced the type size until he was reading typical type (12 point).

Within three years of near-daily teaching, my son was an independent reader. I have to wonder if my misguided use of huge type in the personal books made a significant difference in his speed of learning. If I were starting all over again, I'd deliberately make the same "mistake."

Drive a Truck through It

Almost as important as the size of the type is the *space between each word.* I would be thrilled if you could drive a truck through the spaces you allow in your emergent reader materials. At a minimum, you need *two spaces* between words.

This can be hard to remember as you're typing the text on the computer, but double-check your work: leave two or three spaces between each word.

I have copies of some of the United Kingdom's *Peter and Jane* emergent reader series. Until not many years ago, this was a standard series used to teach reading in the UK. The very first books have *four spaces* between words. You could indeed drive a truck between them.

Why is this extra space important? Because when we use this technique, we eliminate an unnecessary task for the brain: it no longer has to solve the question of "where does that first word end, and where does the next one start?" We've made separation and delineation very clear and have eliminated one brain task by isolating the word with white space.

Since our goal in teaching reading—in all its aspects—is to *make the job easy*, this is an adjustment we can make with no cost or extra effort beyond remembering to hit the space bar two or three times between each word.

Use a Sans Serif Font

What's a sans serif ("without serif) font? It's a font with no curlicues on the ends of letters. The letters are formed with straight lines and simple curves much as most of us learned to print our letters in elementary school. A serif font, in contrast, has extra ornaments and curves. It's fancier, but also harder for a beginner to read. This book is set in a serif font because it's appropriate for books that are intended for proficient readers. The font types we see on the Internet are predominately sans serif. Why? *Because it's easy to read, and people want you to buy their stuff.* So the online czars make it easy for you by the ubiquitous use of sans serif fonts. Let's learn from them.

Interestingly, the *Peter and Jane* series I just mentioned was not only brilliantly spaced; it was also set in a sans serif font. That was unusual for the time. Here in the United States, we were using the *Dick and Jane* series, which was always set in a serif font. Some designers in the United Kingdom certainly knew what they were doing!

Here is an example of Verdana, 12 pt.
And this is Tahoma, 12 pt.
Arial looks like this in 12 pt.
And Helvetica looks like this in 12 pt.

Here is a visual comparison of a serif font in 12 point (too small) versus sans serif (Arial) at 24 point with double spacing, which is a minimum size for making reading easier:

Tommy found a shaggy dog. He named her Floppy.

Tommy found
a shaggy dog.
He named her Floppy.

There are other sans serif fonts as well, but chances are very high that your computer has most of these fonts, as they are standard. This is one more gift we can give the brain, one more way of making its task easier, as it tries to make sense of what it sees on a page.

White Space Is the Learner's Friend

Graphic designers know the value of white space. White space offers visual relief and tells the brain where to look and where not to look. For this reason, we surround the line of type with plenty of white space—and in the beginning stages of teaching, we leave the left-hand pages blank. The student knows exactly where to look: we have, without saying anything, directed him to the line(s) of type on the right-hand page. If you learn to use white space well, even later when you're using longer blocks of type and more pictures, you'll still be helping the brain and telling it where to look.

Don't Give the Words Competition

Graphic designers are trained to design the printed page in a manner that controls the reader's eye and perception. The eye is, in fact, told where to go. The reader has no options; his eyes will go where they are visually directed. If we keep this in mind when we design reading material for our learners, we can enhance learning speed immeasurably.

One of the most important elements in the very beginning of teaching emergent readers is this: *put no pictures on the same visual field as the text.* When readers are more advanced and have success and experience under their belts, then we can juxtapose picture with text; until then, we only slow down the learning process if we use the two together. We use the pictures separately in the early stages of teaching reading, as I explained in the previous chapter.

Win-win

Following the simple guidelines in this chapter will enable you to give the student's ability and willingness to learn a tremendous boost. Making it easier for the brain results in faster success, and with success comes enthusiasm and confidence. Designing for the brain is a completely win-win arrangement.

CHAPTER 6

Teaching to the Brain

Neurology of Learning

"Reading is a brain function; spelling is a set of rules." With these words written in 1963, Glenn Doman tried to highlight the difference in how these two learning tasks should be approached. The fact that reading is indeed a brain function and not a set of rules is now being proved and expanded on by extensive research done in the emerging field of the neurology of learning. To quote Professor Stanislas Dehaene in his talk *How the Brain Learns to Read* (YouTube), "We can say that reading consists essentially of creating an interface between vision and the spoken language system. The child already has a language system and visual system; but [the brain] needs to create an interface." If you want to spend a fascinating evening of reading, just park yourself in front of your computer and Google "neurology of learning."

Largely because of technological advancements, neurology (the branch of medicine that deals with the anatomy, function, and disorders of the nervous system) continues to be a rapidly expanding field of knowledge. And thankfully, the neurology of learning has become a new focus for development. We now have the technical ability to discover and measure things that

Doman could only dream of. But he was correct: reading is a brain function, and this will inform the way we teach our learners to read.

Neuromodulators: Classroom Cheering Squad

To understand how important it is to "go in through the heart," it's worth taking a look at Dr. Martha Burns's TEDx talk on *The New Brain Science of Learning*, which was just one talk in a symposium on education. Because of research into the neurology of learning, we've now got valuable data that backs up anecdotal evidence. When I admonish parents and educators to "go in through the heart" and explain that targeting a child's favorite people, things, and activities opens learning doors wide, we now know neurologically *why that works*.

Dr. Burns talks about the *what* of teaching and the *how* of teaching. The *what* concerns such elements as symbol development, reading, math, and sciences, and involves educating the left hemisphere of the brain.

The *how* of teaching is what keeps the learner engaged, motivated, interactive, and excited. "Going in through the heart" with learner-specific materials plays right into the *how* category. It gets three critical neurotransmitters (brain chemicals) partying. I call these neuromodulators–dopamine, acetylcholine, and norepinephrine—the classroom cheering squad.

When learning is *fun*, **dopamine** is released—a definite plus for the student, as dopamine can be rightly dubbed the "happy hormone." Dr. Burns calls dopamine's effect the "save" button in the brain's computer: with the release of dopamine, the knowledge begins to solidify.

Acetylcholine modulates the attention and alerts the brain when something is important. So if we've created a personal book about a child and his father, the brain is on attention alert: *This is about ME! Me and my daddy!* At this point, the neurons are primed and making new connections, which is what we want.

Norepinephrine (also known as noradrenaline) is released when anything new is introduced. The brain loves novelty (which is why we get hooked into endless Internet surfing and various potential time-sucks like Facebook or YouTube), and that explains why we need to keep fresh materials going in and out of our teaching toolbox. Boredom kills the three squad leaders, so we avoid that at all costs when teaching a child to read.

To keep the brain engaged and those cheering neuromodulators pumping, we use motivating and varied materials, regularly popping something new into the mix, and we move at a good clip to work well with the speed at which the brain likes to learn.

Getting on Speed

If you ask the right brain hemisphere for its personal opinion, it will simply tell you that speed works. Images shown at high speed wake up the right hemisphere, which is highly desirable, since the right brain is responsible for long-term memory storage. The speed at which information can be learned and therefore should be taught is an important element for the learning brain. A quick look at the Right Brain Education Library's website (www.rightbraineducationlibrary. com) is not only fascinating but offers a free membership; the membership gives you access to a manual as well as super-high-speed teaching downloads.

The Doman technique (IAHP) as well as the Shichida and Heguru methods (both founded in Japan) brought to light the fact that the brains of even very small children like to learn *extremely quickly*. This finding had an enormous impact on the development of the technique we now know as Fast Flash.

If you show a flash card to a child slowly, her brain has already shifted into boredom. Flashing two cards per second—or at the very least, one card per second—works extremely well with brain synapses (a synapse is a region or gap across which information from one neuron flows to another). If you doubt that the brain craves speed, just try the Fast Flash method of teaching words by sight, and you'll be convinced by the results. Slow = boredom and sluggish brain absorption. Boredom dramatically reduces the release of those three neuromodulators that we know are essential for learning.

As I was speaking about this "fast phenomenon" in a workshop once, a dad raised his hand and volunteered a story. "I was trying to teach my son to read with flash cards. I held up a card that said BALL. 'This is BALL, Jimmy.' I said. 'B-b-b-b-ball. BALL. What else starts with B?' Rolling his eyes, my son said, '*Boring*.'"

We now know much more effective ways to engage the brain's attention, and speed is one important component.

Repetition and the Brain's Superhighway

I have already talked about frequency of teaching reading and how important frequency and repetition are to the development of the myelin sheath. It bears repeating. There are neural highways of connections in the brain, as we know. Long fiber tracks are typically laid down in the first year or so of life. Dr. Burns calls these tracks "superhighways" and explains, "The more you use the highway, the more you practice a skill, the thicker the myelin gets, and the better you get at that skill, and the faster it goes." Repetition is essential for our learners, even more so than it is for neurotypical learners. Practice, practice, practice thickens the myelin sheath.

Working Memory Games

Anything that we can do to strengthen working memory is a plus; one way we can stretch that working memory is with memory games. Any simple, clear apps that offer memory games are good tools to use. Simpler still is a tabletop card game you can play with picture cards. I use this game not only as a help to develop working memory but also as an excellent intake assessment tool in determining where a student might need help. If working memory is weak, a child will have a harder time learning to read. If that's the case with your child, you'll want to focus on strengthening it. I'll spell out the steps here to a simple memory game; you can also view this on YouTube as I practice it with a student (see the references at the end of the book).

The setup for the card game is simple:

1. Place up to seven pictures of objects (objects well known to your child) face down on the table. Place them in a line and work from the child's left to right, as we do in reading.

2. Turn up the first card and have the child name the object. (Alternatively, she can sign the word or give a verbal approximation).

3. Turn the card face down again. Tap the card and ask, "What was that?"

4. After she gives the answer, turn up both that card and the next card in line. Ask her to name the new object. Then turn both cards face down. Now she has two to remember. Ask her to name them.

5. As she names each card correctly, turn each card face up. While those are still face up, turn up the next card in line. Have her name the new object and then turn all of the cards face down.

6. Ask her now to name each face-down card she's already seen. As she names each, turn it face up. Then turn up a new card and ask her to name the object.

7. Continue in this way until all the cards are shown and remembered. Here's an example of the beginning steps of the game:

Whole Child Reading

Teaching Setup and Tools for Focus

When teaching, sitting *across from* —not alongside—the student is the optimum position, for the simple reason that you can see the learner's eyes. Her eyes may be anywhere except where they need to be, and sitting across from her puts you on top of that problem. For a parent especially, this helps your child make an important psychological shift: Mommy (or Daddy) sitting beside me and snuggling at bedtime read-aloud is different from Mom-or-Dad-as-teacher sitting directly across from me and teaching me to read. And it reminds you that you must monitor your child's focus and learning.

Pointers

Another focusing help is the use of pointers, unsharpened pencils of colorful design. I've got pencils with patterns of footballs, soccer balls, hearts, music—you name it. The more colorful, the better, and of course the student picks her own choice for the day (and typically picks one for me, too); we both use our own pointers. This nifty tool has these benefits:

1. A pointer enables you to see where the student is—or is not—and makes it simple to point out the correct word.

2. It keeps you from having to give negative verbal cues ("No, we're on *ball* now..."). Instead, you can simply pick up the eraser end of the pencil and move it to the correct word.

3. Your own pointer guides the reader to the correct words as well.

4. Using a pointer keeps little hands busy.

5. A colorful pointer keeps corrections impersonal and much more fun than seeing teacher's finger-in-your-face move across the page.

6. Using pointers instead of their own fingers keeps children's faces at the correct distance from the page; "nose to page" is a hard habit to break once it's engrained.

Good reading position.

Avoid nose-to-paper habit

No Distractions

It goes without saying that the teaching area should be free of distractions, both visual and audible. No radio or TV going on within earshot; no classmates or siblings distracting; no iPad, iPhone, or toys in sight, etc. If the learner is agitated, dim the lights...and avoid fluorescent lighting. Studies have been done on the negative effects of fluorescent lighting on humans of all sizes—more than enough to warrant avoiding them when possible.

Dim the Lights

Dimming the lights for a student with an autism spectrum disorder (ASD) can have a very calming effect. I routinely use dim incandescent lamps with any student who seems agitated, overstimulated, or especially tired. My students give me much more cooperation when I create a more soothing environment.

Flashlight Pens

Typically if I dim the lights, I also offer the student a flashlight pen to use as we read. I use one as well; this substitutes for a pointer when the lights are dimmed. Flashlight pens, as you probably anticipate, are a popular item in reading sessions. It's a good motivator and puts the learner "in charge," which is always a plus.

Job Description: Patience Required

I often hear exasperated complaints along these lines: "But she doesn't retain the words I teach her! She knew these three words on Monday, but on Tuesday, she acts like she's never seen them before!"

Right. This is normal, we expect this, and all is well in our world. This will be the case until the information is successfully and permanently stored in long-term memory. Speed and repetition will get the job done, and that's why we use the Fast Flash method and teach those "five minutes twice a day" that I'll talk about later. One day, those forgotten words will stay and never leave, making reading effortless. Which brings us to the topic of the jungle...

The Jungle of the Visual Pathway

I briefly mentioned the all-important visual pathway when I talked about designing for the brain. Let's take a closer look at it now.

You can think of the visual pathway as a dense jungle, overgrown and impossible to find a pathway through. That, if you will, is the scene that you face when you begin to teach reading to someone with an immature or underdeveloped visual pathway. We're not talking about actual sight ability here. A thirty-year-old who is not yet reading may have 20/20 vision but still have an immature visual pathway, and the process of teaching her to read will involve gradually maturing that pathway.

Recognizing a Domino Pizza marquee is a continent away from recognizing that tiny black squiggles on a page tell a marvelous story. To again pluck a quote from a letter written to me by Greg Czarnecki, the educator who started me on this road in 1990: "The ability to read is a significant human skill. People underestimate the mental, visual, and muscle coordination necessary to change abstractions on paper into meaningful thoughts. A miracle occurs when it happens."

So as we're pursuing this miracle, using the speed of Fast Flash and the repetition of "five minutes twice a day," we are helping to forge a pathway through the jungle. At first, it seems that all the work we did the previous day has vanished, and the jungle is just as dense as it was before; but little by little, that information sticks and we clear a pathway through the jungle. Eventually, the student knows those words every day of the week, not just on Monday. That information has made the successful journey into long-term memory, largely because of our focus on speed and right brain learning, which controls long-term memory.

Brain Exercises

I begin my teaching sessions with some brain-prepping time. My weekly time with students has to be maximized, and doing brain exercises before teaching gives me the best possible chance of making an impact. I also include some confidence-boosting rituals, as many, if not most, learners with special needs thrive on predictability, routine, and encouragement.

Cross-Crawl Exercise

I highly recommend Dr. Paul Dennison's book, *Brain Gym and Me*. Once a struggling fourth grader, Dr. Dennison went on to develop simple physical exercises that target particular learning difficulties and help the student to overcome them. I consider the cross-crawl exercise the most important, and if you have no time to do any other Brain Gym exercises, this is the one to use.

Why do the cross-crawl? What does it do? The goal of this exercise is to coordinate both hemispheres working together. The right brain hemisphere controls the left side of the body; the left hemisphere controls the right side of the body. If we do this exercise correctly, we enable coordination between both hemispheres. We need strong midfield or central vision for reading, and this exercise helps engage the whole brain so we can access midfield vision, among other marvelous brain effects.

The exercise is done in a way that simulates marching in place. It's simple to do, and a video is indeed worth more than a thousand words (see the References for a YouTube suggestion).

To do the cross-crawl correctly, only two things need to happen to effectively to integrate both the right and left hemispheres of the brain:

1. One limb must cross midline in the body (visualize an imaginary line down the center of the body; that's your "midline")...

2. while an opposing limb (on opposite side of the body) *moves*. It doesn't cross midline; it just moves, meaning that the hemisphere connected with that limb is activated.

So what does this look like? For example, your right hand crosses over midline on your body and taps your left knee as your left leg rises to meet your hand (like marching). Then your left hand does the same "tap" on your right knee as you continue marching. That's it.

There are a number of creative variations on this if you want to get fancy. As I mentioned, the Appendix lists a good URL to get you started with cross-crawl.

With each tap of the knee counting as "one," I suggest this formula, taught me by Ann Anzalone years ago (www.annanzalone.com). I often refer to Ann as "the Brain Lady," and with good reason. Here is the sequence that I used daily with my son and that I now use in my workshops, subjecting all attendees to this mandatory "do-it-now-so-you'll-get-it-in-your-muscle-memory" exercise:

24 Cross-crawls (each opposing knee tap counting as one)
10 Knee taps *same-side*-hand-to-*same-side*-knee
24 Cross-crawls (each opposing knee tap counting as one)
10 Knee taps *same-side*-hand-to-*same-side*-knee
24 Cross-crawls (each opposing knee tap counting as one)

The sequences of ten knee taps with "left hand to left knee" and "right hand to right knee," though not technically a cross-crawl exercise, are an important part of this system, as it allows the body to regroup in a brief few moments of homeostasis. Then we dive right back into crossing midline and connecting the two brain hemispheres with the twenty-four cross-crawls, ending with the cross-crawl sequence.

Why do this instead of just, let's say, twenty-four or forty-eight cross-crawls? The proof is in the pudding: I've done it both ways in workshops over the years. If I ask the audience to stand and do twenty-four cross-crawls, everyone does it and then quietly sits back down in their chairs.

If I ask the audience to stand and do the 24-10-24-10-24 sequence as I outlined it above, when we finish, the audience *invariably* breaks into bubbly laughter and happy chatter. It happens *every single time*. Can I tell you why there is such a difference when the sequence is done this way? No. You might have to ask the Brain Lady about that. Just know that it does and follow that sequence.

Children who can't do the routine comfortably in a standing position can do it in a chair. Babies can sit in your lap, with you assisting by doing hand-over-hand and lifting leg-under-leg.

These two pictures can give you an idea, but do watch the YouTube video suggested in the Appendix.

Super Brain Yoga

Super Brain Yoga is a second exercise that I consider invaluable for doing the same thing—integrating the right and left hemispheres of the brain as well as additionally stimulating neural pathways in the brain. You can see it demonstrated on YouTube, where it is listed as "Super Brain Yoga." A good starting video is listed in the References. This video includes testimonials from several special education teachers, and went viral some years ago. Around that same time, I happened to be watching the Winter Olympics and the camera caught one of the luge Olympians warming up for his competition by practicing Super Brain Yoga in front of millions of global TV watchers. How's that for a recommendation?

Directions for doing this exercise are simple:

1. Left hand grips the lower right earlobe.

2. Right hand grips the lower left earlobe.

3. Right arm should be on top.

4. Grip the ear lobes (this activates hundreds of acupressure points).

5. Inhale while you bend the knees going down.

6. Exhale as you straighten your legs coming up.

7. Do this slowly (don't race through them) for a minute or more if you can, at least fourteen times.

For those more deeply interested in the effect that simple physical exercises can have on the brain, I encourage you to explore Dr. Dennison's book, *Brain Gym and Me* (see Appendix). In my son's school years, the cross-crawl exercise alone had such a positive impact on his behavior that I did it with him every morning before he got on the school bus. The effect on brain

organization lasts approximately four hours, so I recommend that educators do either of these exercises with their class the first thing in the school day and then again after lunch.

Music for the Brain and How to Use It

In 1997, Don Campbell wrote a mind-blowing book, *The Mozart Effect: Tapping the Power of Music*, which advocated for using music to promote learning and healing. Many publishers jumped on the bandwagon, and today you have more choices for purchasing "music for the brain" than you would ever want to buy. Not all are of the best quality. For many years, I kept my website well supplied with what I consider the best music for learning. Published by the LIND Institute in San Francisco, all of the selections were very carefully researched. But when the Danish founder, Ole Anderson, decided to retire and return to the homeland, that resource dried up.

However, used copies of an invaluable guide written by Anderson can still be found online on sites such as Amazon and Barnes and Noble. I suggest you pursue getting a copy if this topic interests you. The book is titled *Learn with the Classics: Using Music to Study Smart at Any Age*. In it, Anderson outlines the best way to select and use music optimally for learning. Here is the core information:

■ **Entrainment.** There is a process of "brain entrainment" that we can use to our advantage with the appropriate type of music. This definition from www.bestbinauralbeats.org explains it well: "Brain entrainment is the name for utilizing sound to create positive changes in your mental or even physical performance." These changes can include relaxation of breaths and heartbeats as well as beneficial changes in brain waves.

- **55–70 beats per minute.** Optimum entrainment for the brain's capacity to learn occurs when the music—if it's carefully selected—has between 55 and 70 beats per minute, which is the ideal pulse rate at rest for humans. Listening to this music, we begin to relax and yet remain alert, achieving what Anderson terms "active relaxation." We want this state for learning!

- **Alpha and Beta Brainwaves.** *Beta* is the active state. When we're studying, for example, we are in beta. But long-term memory storage happens in the *alpha* state of "active relaxation." The classical music recommended by Anderson provides us with both, depending on the volume of the music. Some highly recommended examples from Mozart are the *Romance* from his *Eine Kleine Nachtmusik (A Little Night Music),* the *Adagio* from his opera *Die Zauberflote (The Magic Flute),* and the *Andante* from his *Piano Concerto No. 15.* If you listen to any of those selections, you'll have a very good idea of the kind of music and tempo you're looking for.

- **Volume for beta.** Played very softly as we study or teach, this music helps keep us in the focused or beta state. How softly should you play the music during the teaching time? So softly that the student doesn't notice it. The brain, however, will register it. That's all you want during teaching time. If you or the student *notices* the music playing during teaching, it's too loud. Turn it down.

- **Volume for alpha.** But to get the information we're teaching or studying into long-term memory, we want to get our learners into the alpha or actively relaxed state. You can encourage this state by playing the music at a comfortably louder and enjoyable volume both before you teach (while you're both getting ready for the session) and again when teaching is finished.

- **Attracting both brain hemispheres.** Taking Mozart's music as an example, we are able to achieve a greater "whole brain" state when listening to it because the beauty of melodic lines engages the creative right hemisphere of the brain while the precise mathematics of this orderly music engages the left hemisphere. That's the *why* of choosing Mozart, for example. Not all music contains such hidden mathematical precision; Johann Sebastian Bach did it superbly as well.

- **Shifting between alpha and beta.** I'll let Ole Anderson continue: "When you are studying…you will have the music on very low, so your brain will stay in the 'doing' state of beta, the thinking state…When you take breaks for reflection, turn the music up and become more attentive to it. You will shift to your creative alpha state. *It is the music's ability to shift your brain between alpha and beta that primes your brain for learning.*"

While I can't personally recommend products available now, I suggest that a good choice would probably be one of the many CDs and CD sets now produced by Don Campbell, the author of the book that first awakened the public to the power of music's effect on the brain. Just remember that not just *any* music by Mozart (or classical music) will have the desired effect. Keep in mind Ole Anderson's guide of using music that has between 55 and 70 beats per minute, and listen to the classical music samples I recommended; those can be your yardstick for purchasing similarly effective music.

Beloved Rituals

This next teaching suggestion is one that engages both heart and brain: establish a beginning ritual for your teaching sessions. Our children seem to love not only predictability but also rituals. Pleasant rituals that engage multiple senses are an effective way to start a teaching session, because they not only prime the brain for learning but also help the child to anticipate the learning mind-set just ahead—like waving a "get ready to focus!" flag.

I have had parents report that their children spontaneously practice parts of my beginning brain-priming ritual anywhere, any time. Know for certain that these children would not voluntarily do these exercises if it didn't make them feel better!

Some years ago, I observed an extraordinary teacher in Southern California, Terry Stanton Brown. Devoted to teaching only individuals with Down syndrome, Terry begins each session with a multisensory brain-and-spirit boost. I liked her inclusion of both Emotional Freedom Tapping (I'll explain that in a minute) and what she calls "focus spray," and I have incorporated both into my beginning ritual ever since.

What does my own ritual look like?

1. We sit across from each other on a cheerful yoga mat.

2. I hold up a foot-wide brass gong, and the student signals the start of our session by hitting it with a padded mallet (multiple times, until she's satisfied—or my ears give out.)

3. We use a "focus spray" of essential oils mixed with water in a spritzer. The student chooses both the fragrance and the number of squirts of the spray, but I am the one controlling the spray bottle, as I want to make

sure the spray goes up in the air and not in anyone's eyes!

4. We enjoy the fragrance, inhale it deeply, and begin Emotional Freedom Tapping (EFT). In a nutshell, this involves tapping on certain meridian points on the head and body while we affirm wonderful things such as these: "I'm smart," "I'm focused," "I'm a good learner," "I love books!" etc. Tapping is done on many places: on the top of the head, over the eyebrows, under the eyes, etc. For more details, do an Internet search on "emotional freedom tapping" or "EFT."

5. Then it's stand-up time: time for Brain Gym's cross-crawl exercise, Super Brain Yoga, or both.

6. We move to a narrow table (narrow so that I'm close to the student as I sit across from her) and start our reading session.

Two ritual stories:

■ One of my teenaged students with Down syndrome was too afraid initially to hit the gong. Because of both fine and gross motor challenges, she couldn't quite figure out how to position her arm to give the gong a good whack. Today she hits it out of the park at decibel levels near the legal limits. *That's* progress.

■ A student with difficult behavior, whose parents are pursuing some quality applied behavior analysis (ABA) intervention, came in for his lesson in a very bad mood. He'd been in a bad mood all day, his mother reported. He sat with his black hoodie pulled completely over his head and face, howling his objection. So I brought his parents into my session room too. We played the game of Dad and Mom first having to do Super Brain Yoga. "Now your turn!" I said to him. Nope, he was having none of it. Then I tried EFT. As I coached his father through his turn, the child—*through his hoodie*—began to tap his own head. He is one of those children who had been observed spontaneously doing EFT on his own; somehow, he understands that it helps him feel better, and almost against his will, he began to do it with us. That turned the tide, and I was eventually able to get his cooperation in the teaching session.

I absolutely recommend using a beginning ritual of your choice because 1) it feels good to the student, 2) it elicits cooperation, 3) it helps the brain and heart, and 4) predictability is a help to children with developmental delays. It is quite literally a preparatory tool for learning. So pick and choose among good brain aids such as I've outlined here, and add your own creative touch. You'll be pleased with the results!

Praise, the Final Brain Boost

Speaking of generating essential neuromodulators, praise will do it. The more encouragement and sincere praise we give our children, the better they perform. In any skill—academic or sport—confidence is essential, and encouragement helps build confidence.

If you haven't seen any of the online videos of special education teacher Christopher Ulmer of Jacksonville, Florida, take a look at his Facebook page, "Special Books by Special Kids." Some of Chris's videos have gone viral, in particular the one where he spends the *first ten minutes of each school day* (definitely classifies as a "beginning ritual") praising each of his students individually. (On YouTube, you can search for "Special Ed Teacher Compliments Students.") Within a few weeks of beginning his "praise practice," Chris was thrilled to see that all of the students began praising and encouraging *each other*. I think it's safe to say that the entire class has gotten a brain boost from this practice.

I have tutored students who have been raised on self-confidence and encouragement, and it shows in their own self-congratulations, which pop up from time to time as they "self-talk" in our sessions: "Good job, Blair!" "Good job, Makenna!" Makenna, in fact, once turned that praise around in our session and said to me, "Good job, Ma-la-lee!" I discovered in that moment that none of us is ever beyond enjoying encouragement, teacher included!

CHAPTER

7

Modifying Trade Books

The Bee's Knees

Modified trade books are the other half of "going in through the heart," personal books being the first half. Modified books are adored by our students *because they look just like the books their typical peers are reading*...and our kids can read them! This is a powerful self-esteem boost and an inclusion tool as well.

What Exactly Are Trade Books?

Trade books are (usually paperback) books for children/teens that you'll find in sizeable bookstores or the book department of any StuffMart store: Walmart, Kmart, and Target, to name the primary "marts." You can also look online (Amazon, eBay, etc.) We are particularly interested in the trade books for early readers—and especially those focusing on the latest popular movies or TV shows or other topics of high interest to our learners. Movie-related reading books are always released just before the movies are and may or may not be available for a couple of months afterward. Past that time, you'll need to search online booksellers for those titles, so it pays to peruse those stores at movie-release time.

Can you trust the "level" indication on the cover of any of these trade books, regardless of publisher? No.

There is absolutely *no quality control* in the trade book industry requiring claims on the cover to be in line with the actual reading level within the covers. The cover icon may say "Pre-Reading," and the interior text can be third-grade level. I've seen this mismatch between claimed and actual reading level too often; trust my experience with this and spare yourself spending money on books you can't use. As long as you can "look inside" online or actually physically look at a few *interior* pages, you'll be able to make good choices.

So which publisher does the closest job of matching actual interior text to the advertised reading level as marked on the cover, give or take a level? Random House in its "Step Into Reading" series. This line of reading books is standardly found in bookstores and the marts I mentioned, and is easily recognized by the dark blue banner at the top of the book covers. Typically, you can find reading levels 1, 2, and sometimes 3 in stores. Here's a visual help:

I suggest you explore that series and go from there, doing your own research on books your child will find of high interest.

What Do You Mean by Modifying Books?

You're going to change the text in these books. You'll rewrite the text according to the skill level of your learner, stretching him only a bit: enough to help him progress, but not enough to discourage him. Once you've rewritten the text, you'll type it on full-label sheets (any office store has these), cut the sheet to match the space on the page, and permanently affix it to the page. You'll modify the entire book this way, and in the end you'll have created a popular reading book that your learner can proudly master.

These modified books are extremely high motivators. And as with the topics selected for personal books, you will want to choose *only* trade books on topics your learner loves. At the earliest stages of enticing an emergent reader to love reading and books, we avoid modifying books that *we* think will be good for him or that *we'd* like him to be interested in. That defeats the purpose at this early stage. We want the emergent reader to read for content, to be excited about what he is reading, and to eventually fall in love with reading. At this early point, our learners direct our topic choice.

Are there any books that *don't* qualify as good candidates for modification? Yes. In that category would be books already known and loved by the child, as well as classics such as *The Very Hungry Caterpillar, If You Give a Mouse a Cookie,* etc. Your child will object to your messing with the original versions of books he has probably memorized, and many classic books just don't lend themselves to rewriting. They're perfect as they are and don't modify in a satisfying way. So you'll pick a *new* book to modify.

How Do We Modify?

To modify trade books, you'll use the know-how you gained in chapter 4 on "Personal Books." All of the technical aspects are the same: font size, font type, double/triple spacing between words, age-level topics, appropriate reading level (vocabulary, sentence length, number of sentences on a page), etc. All of this remains the same. Here are the steps you'll want to follow:

1. **Choose a *new* trade book**—one that your child *has not seen* yet but would love (see my comment above: no well-loved or classic books).

2. **Ensure that the book's topic is of *high* interest to your child.** Note that the **high-interest** words are already selected for you because of the book's topic. No need to make a high-interest word list. You'll be working with the content on each page of the book.

3. **Select high-frequency words to use.** As I just mentioned, you won't need a high-interest word list when you modify a trade book; but you will need a high-*frequency* word list. So take another look at the Dolch or Fry word lists you worked with when you made personal books. As you did then, target a word list level that your learner hasn't yet mastered. You might decide on which of these words you'd like to use repeatedly within the story line of the book. Make a list of these and keep them handy.

4. **Stop. Write down the age and reading level of the learner.** I'm repeating this from the chapter on creating personal books, because it's equally important here: *don't go any further until you've done this ten-second bit of work.* As I mentioned before, in my reading workshops, I often see attendees waste their workshop time when they forge ahead without figuring this out first. Backtracking takes time that you don't have.

5. **Based on that age and level, decide the format specifics.** To repeat my advice from the instructions for personal books, decide how long your sentences should be, how large the type should be, and how much text you should put on a page.

a. **Emergent reading level** (regardless of age, the student is at the earliest stages of reading—that is, he is learning letter sounds and the first 40+ sight words.) Use three- or four-word sentences and one sentence to a page. Font size depends on how much space you have to work with on each page. Keep the font size consistent throughout the book; don't change font size from page to page just because the available space changes. Keep the font size the same.

b. **Pre-primer or primer reading level** (the reader is in the process of mastering the first two Dolch word lists or the first Fry list along with many content words). Use five- to six-word sentences, one or two sentences to a page. Follow the font size guidelines described in (a).

c. **First-grade reading level** (the reader is in the process of mastering the first-grade Dolch list or the second Fry word list, gaining fluency and speed). Write longer sentences, several sentences to a page. Follow the same font size guidelines described in (a).

6. **Stick to that format! Don't vary it. *Be consistent.*** Remember not to mix up the format, randomly abandoning the "age + reading level" formula you've already taken the time to think through.

7. **Rewrite the text on each page.** You might want to use larger stick-on notes for this job while you're rewriting and editing your new text. Write the new text on the stick-on note and affix it to the page. You will use removable notes at this stage because you may want to change the text before you've finished revising the book.

a. **Cover the text on each page** with your hand first and take a look at what you see. Why? Because the illustration that remains is all the child will see when you've modified the book. You're going to be covering the original text.

b. Decide what the illustration is telling the child.

c. Write new text with *that* in mind. Never mind what the original text actually said, because the child is going to see only the picture and your text.

8. **Type the new text on full-label sheets.** Measure the amount of space (the width and height in inches) available for placing text on each page; type the text within those parameters. As I mentioned, use "full label sheets" purchased at an office supply store. Cut out the text area on the label when you've printed it and affix it to the corresponding page. This is a permanent arrangement; adhesive labels cannot be removed. One nifty idea is to purchase two copies of the book—if it's an absolute favorite topic for your child—and save one copy untouched for him to enjoy later when he reaches a more advanced level.

9. **Make flash cards for all the essential words.** Typically, modified books have far more vocabulary than personal books. So you'll want to pick and choose: Which are the most important words for the student to learn first? Create those cards according to the same instructions in the chapter 4. I recommend creating actual flash cards (see directions on Fast Flash), but if you're inclined to skip the printing of cards, look in that same section and review tips on using iPad apps to create electronic flash cards.

10. **Teach "Sandwich Style" and test with Errorless Testing Techniques.** (See chapters 8 and 9 for information on those two topics.)

Shopping Tips

It helps to know what you're looking for when you shop for books, so here is a quick list of ideal book characteristics:

1. High-interest topics only

2. Clear page layout: no clutter or confusing visuals

3. Small text blocks that you can easily cover. If the text is scattered around the page, as it sometimes is in picture books, it will be difficult, if not distracting, to cover with new text.

Sample Makeover Tutorial

I wish I could show you before and after samples of pages that I've actually modified for students with Down syndrome and other disabilities so that I could talk about why they didn't work as printed and what I did to make them work beautifully for my learners. But copyright laws don't smile indulgently on me taking awesome Disney/Pixar movie books, giving them an overhaul, and printing samples of those in a book that they didn't publish.

So here are some fictitious examples I concocted, with brain-unfriendly errors I frequently see in trade books. Let's look at the problems and the solutions.

Example 1: Pigs

These pigs look like Babe, don't they?
Pigs live on a farm and like to dig for
worms and bugs. Little piglets are cute.

Let's analyze the errors in this sample from our hypothetical reading book. What's wrong with it? Let me count the ways…

1. White type on a dark background is hard to read and tiring for the brain.

2. The type is miniscule and in a serif font rather than a sans serif font.

3. All the child sees is the huge picture; the brain is captivated and is not interested in the tiny type.

So how can we modify this to work well? Here are several options:

1. In this first "fix," designed for an emergent reader, I've covered the type with a label so the new text pops out in spite of the predominance of the large illustration.

2. If I were modifying this for a learner at a higher reading level, primer level, for example, I might do this:

Even though the photograph is dominant in this example, the modification still makes it easier for the learner to see and attend to the text. Note that in all these examples of modification, I stick to the brain-friendly format of sans serif type, large font size, double spacing between each word, and extra leading between lines of type.

Example 2: I like to read

You think I'm making this problem up? I'm not. I see this black-type-against-a-dark-background frequently in trade books. I have no clue what publishers are thinking when they create a "reading book" like this. So what's the problem with this sample?

1. The text is unreadable.
2. The text is a serif font.

3. Spacing between words is too tight.

The good news in this example is that the actual level of the text, in this case, is fine. No need to do any rewriting if the reader is at least at a primer level. So how can we fix the problems? This one's easy. We use a permanent label, as we always do, to cover the original text; and we type the same text in a sans serif font, using double-spacing between words and extra leading between lines. Here's our new reading book:

Example 3: Bake a cake

In this example, visibility of text is good. All we need to do is rewrite the text at the level of our learner and put it in a brain-friendly format. Here we go:

My big sister helps me learn to cook. We are baking a cake together. It will taste yummy!

I like to cook.
My big sister
helps me.

A Power Tool

You'll find, after making just one of these modified trade books for your learner, that you've created a powerful motivational tool. Success comes much more easily when the reader loves the topic and the level of difficulty matches the reader's capability. That success is worth every minute spent on modifying these books!

Fast Flash Technique

What's the Fast Flash Technique?

"Fast Flash" is the moniker I use to describe the technique first developed by Glenn Doman. It has been used with wild success for over fifty years by the Institutes for the Achievement of Human Potential and for decades by the National Association for Child Development, as well as by prestigious child development schools of both Shichida method and Heguru schools in Japan, Australia, and around the world. This speedy approach to communicating information to the brain has had a long and successful track record.

The fact that this well-respected technique is not common knowledge and is not taught to every special education teacher should not surprise us. Life presents us with many mysteries, and this is one of them! The fact that the technique is free (corporations can't profit from promoting it) and extremely simple probably doomed its inclusion in fundamental special education tools.

Essential components of this technique when used for children with Down syndrome or other developmental delays are as follows:

1. **Flash cards are literally *flashed*: at least one card per second.**

    a. Flash and name two cards per second if you can manage it.

    b. Essentially, flash and name the cards just as fast as you can move them.

2. **Use red ink if possible.**

    a. Why red? The human brain is attracted to red. This brain preference is well known and used by marketing companies, depending on the product. One motivational speaker was in the habit of asking his adult audiences to silently think of a color; when he asked, "How many of you thought of the color red?" typically half the audience raised their hands.

    b. Test this if you don't believe it (I was skeptical, so I tested it): create two identical flash cards, one in red and one in black, and ask your student which she prefers. You'll see.

3. **Cards are grouped in fives; one, two, or three groups can be taught simultaneously.**

    a. Why five words in a group? Readers with Down syndrome or other developmental delays typically will probably—hopefully—have at least five memory channels in working memory, so a group of five word cards is usually comfortable. (Working memory determines the number of bits of information that we can simultaneously hold and process in our memory.) It is worth experimenting with smaller groups of three or four if you don't see fast learning results with groups of five. Some learners may need fewer cards in a group.

b. People who are neurologically typical may have seven to nine memory channels. Even so, memorization is enhanced by dividing longer digit sequences into smaller ones, which is why phone numbers are grouped in three or four digits. So, keeping our card groups to five words or fewer keeps the task of memorization in a comfortable range.

c. After beginning with one group of cards, add more groups as the learner progresses. Remove words as the student learns them and replace them with new words.

4. **Ratio of high-interest words (H-I) to high-frequency (H-F) words** depends on the receptivity and reading level of the learner.

a. A ratio of two H-I to three H-F words in a group of five is a good start.

b. High frequency words are typically both abstract and boring, especially in the beginning word lists (*in, the, a, am*); peppering the pack with high-interest words is important, especially in early reading stages.

c. With a ratio of two H-I to three H-F words, a typical learner will stay attentive just to see two of her favorite words!

d. An extremely reluctant reader may need a more favorable (to her) ratio, even 4 H-I to 1 H-F. Getting the ratio just right may take some experimenting.

5. **Cards are larger to accommodate large type**.

a. The younger the child or the more immature the visual pathway, the larger the type (even up to two inches high for toddlers).

b. For a toddler, using type this large will necessitate using cut-up tagboard or poster board for flash cards. At any age for a beginning reader, the smallest size I recommend for flash cards is 5" x 8", which is the largest size of index cards available at office supply stores.

c. The visual pathway in an emergent reader is underdeveloped; starting with large letters greatly smoothes the way for its development. Once that refinement begins, smaller and smaller type can be used.

d. Test the size initially by creating two versions of the same word on different flash cards, in two different type sizes. Ask the learner which she prefers and follow that lead.

6. **Cards are flashed as a group three times consecutively as you sit across from the learner.**

a. This should take no more than fifteen seconds total time, and hopefully not more than ten seconds.

b. Handwrite the word on the back of the card so that you see it just before you take the card from the back of the pack and place it in the front of the pack as you name it for the child.

c. Be sure to wait until the card lands in your "showing" hand before you name it. If you say the word *before* it actually lands in your hand for the child to see, the child will be viewing the previous card instead of the one you're naming. This sounds obvious, but I've seen parents make this mistake.

7. **Groups are flashed twice a day.**

a. Frequency, as you've already read, is of prime importance for retention.

8. **Groups/words are changed frequently.**

    a. Material should be fresh, and cards already mastered should be removed from the group; no boredom allowed!

    b. Pull words that are mastered already and replace them with new words.

    c. The teacher's challenge—and fine line to tread—is to infuse fun by introducing new high-interest words while still including the old words not yet mastered. Sometimes you may need to temporarily retire those tired old words and bring them back again later for another try.

9. **Flash the cards by sitting across from the child, not alongside.** Why? So you can see where your child's eyes are; the eyes may be anywhere except on the cards! So, what to do if the child's eyes are wandering?

    a. The most effective alternative I've found is to use the same Fast Flash method, but instead of showing the cards just above eye level, rapidly slap the cards down on the table right beneath the child's nose. I have found that this gets her attention every time. The method is the same: as if you're dealing from a deck of cards, slap/deal the cards rapidly on the table while naming them; then scoop up that group of five cards and repeat that showing twice more.

    b. Remove visual or auditory distractions. For instance, choose your teaching location carefully. The child's bedroom or playroom or TV room are clearly not good choices.

c. Dim the lights just enough to induce a more relaxed learning state; turn off fluorescent lights above and use muted incandescent light. The light in the room should be fully adequate to focus on the cards, but not so bright that it's irritating and puts too much visual emphasis on everything else in the room.

d. Has the child had enough energy-releasing activity before you began the teaching session? Do you need to stop and toss a Koosh ball or something similar?

e. Neuro-Linguistic Programming (NLP) tells us that the optimal eye position for remembering visuals is when the eye of the student is just above the eye's natural horizon line; when you sit across from the learner, it's easy to achieve this level and see that her eyes are looking slightly upward.

10. **The child does *not* repeat the word.**

a. Why not? Because the child has only one job to do during Fast Flash: *to look at the cards.* That's it. We want the brain to absorb what the eye sees.

b. Many children with Down syndrome, autism, or other developmental disabilities have significant speech challenges. The amount of focus and energy that it takes for them to actually *speak* the words as you're naming them would completely derail them from the goal of the moment: *look, listen, and absorb.*

c. In addition, if the child has enough time to repeat the word, you're flashing much too slowly! There should be no time for this.

11. **No testing yet; teaching is not testing.**

a. Teaching is fun, enjoyable, and exciting for the learner; that's our goal.

b. Testing is a separate activity, and we use no-fail "errorless testing techniques" when we do test. (See "Errorless Testing" in chapter 12.)

Why So fast? Isn't That Counterintuitive?

It's because of how the brain retains information best. "To train the right side of the brain, you have to flash as fast as possible." This is the approach of Professors Glenn Doman and Makoto Shichida, both pioneers in the field of child brain development. I highly recommend a walk through this website: www.rightbraineducationlibrary.com. As I've mentioned earlier, with a simple registration of your email address, you'll receive eye-opening information, a manual, and free downloadable flash cards, videos, and more.

When information is given at high speed, the right hemisphere is activated; *long-term memory is a function of the brain's right hemisphere.* This is of course where we want to input the information—into long-term memory. Though neurons fire at different speeds, a neuron can fire about once every 5 milliseconds, or about 200 times a second. We want to hop on the engine at a speed compatible with its movement. Trying to slow the engine down does not enhance learning and easily leads to a loss of interest.

Here's another quote I like: "They are called 'flash' cards for a reason. You should be able to glance at the card and absorb the content in, well, a flash. Research shows that the faster a person can process information, the more likely they are to remember it" (www.respondus.com).

In his book *How to Teach Your Baby to Read,* Doman talks about the brain's preference for learning quickly, a preference that is especially strong in a child's brain—whether there is a developmental delay or not. Doman's seminal work was done entirely with children with either brain injuries or developmental delays—an exact parallel with Maria Montessori, who did very much the same thing, formulating her ingenious teaching methods over two years of teaching children with Down syndrome and other developmental delays. Both Doman and Montessori then turned to the general population to spread their work further, theorizing that if these methods worked so well for seriously challenged children, they could work brilliantly for neurotypical children. They were right.

Don't Believe Me; Just Do It and See for Yourself

As I mentioned at the beginning of this section, this Fast Flash technique is largely unknown within school systems; in my workshops, I encourage educators to simply *do it*. One of my favorite responses, weeks after the workshop, came from one of those educators: "I went back to work and told my colleagues that I was going to use large flash cards with *no pictures* and use the Fast Flash method. They said, 'Sure, like *that's* going to work!' Well, here it is six weeks later, and my entire special ed class has learned fifteen new words solidly. I had been trying to teach them a short list of words for a year with no success. Now my colleagues are saying, 'Wow! That really works!'"

This technique has been successful for decades, and it's absolutely free. Speaking of the brain, this is, truly, a no-brainer.

Where Does Fast Flash Fit into a Teaching Protocol?

You're going to be using Fast Flash in a teaching method I call "Sandwich Style" teaching. Simply put, we flash the cards before reading the material that the words directly relate to (whether a personal book, modified book, classroom book, lotto/matching game, etc.), and we wrap up the teaching session by flashing the cards again. So the "sandwich" is: flash + book + flash.

CHAPTER 9

Sandwich Style Teaching

Make a Sandwich in Five Minutes, Twice a Day

When you first begin to teach, and you're looking at "five minutes twice a day" and wondering what in the world you're going to do within those five minutes, start with "Sandwich Style" teaching. Fast Flash sessions are the two pieces of "bread," and the personal book or any high-interest reading material is the "peanut butter and jelly" in the middle. So the protocol goes like this:

Sandwich Style Teaching

- **Bread:** Fast Flash the select group or groups of words (in groups of five) that the child will need to learn in order to read the book. Flash each group three times, one or two cards per second.

- **Peanut Butter & Jelly:** Read the personal book or other high-interest material together. As the child progresses, the teacher drops out gradually, with the child eventually reading all the words. For a child struggling with speech, alternatives to saying the word aloud are signing or any *consistent* verbal approximation. In the latter case, the accuracy of the sound doesn't matter; what matters is consistency of the specific sound produced for a particular word.

■ **Bread:** Fast Flash the *same* select group or groups of words (in groups of five) that you flashed before reading the book/ material. Fast Flash each group three times.

Be sure that the PB&J doesn't come across more like sand-choked spinach. In other words, make sure that the reward between those slices of Fast Flash is a *real* reward: fun, of high interest, and well liked by the reader.

Then What?

Following that, for whatever amount of time your learner can now sit for (this will increase with time), mix and match from the following activities, most of which are addressed in the remaining chapters:

■ introduction of new material

■ errorless testing

■ phonics work

■ decoding work, especially based on errors (words missed) in the "PB&J" part of the session

■ fluency/speed work

■ comprehension work

Each session may be a combination of any of those elements. We have to repeat unlearned material, but to avoid the risk of boredom, we introduce a variety of work. Keep the material fresh.

As I've mentioned previously, five minutes is just the start. You will increase the time as your child's success, confidence, and enthusiasm build. Then gradually expanding that time will seem natural and comfortable.

Please refer to the final chapter, which outlines a step-by-step teaching protocol for you to follow. Within that natural progression, you have options and can introduce the variety of materials and methods that your child needs.

Balancing Old and New

The trickiest teaching challenge, the "razor's edge" of teaching reading, is probably this: we need to balance the need to introduce fresh material with the necessity of teaching old material not mastered. One mother summed up the typical questions parents have: *"My child is three, and we're having fun using your program. When do I add new books? When I think she's getting bored? How do we review the old ones and do both new and old in five minutes twice a day? I'm having trouble keeping it straight."*

Teaching is primarily intuitive, building naturally on the knowledge base of the educator. This intuitive element is even more important in teaching children with delays, as it seems that many—if not most of them—are highly intuitive, and operate very well on that frequency. If you can tune in to them, you will know the answers to those questions on the spot. But here are some suggestions in response to that mother's questions.

Q. When do I add new books?
A. Keep a balance of fresh material flowing in; I've mentioned that the brain loves novelty—anything new is going to merit its attention. When the child is able to read 90 percent of the

book, it's fine to create a new book. But keep the older book in the "review" stack so that it can be mastered. A simple way to help that happen is to repeat unlearned vocabulary in the next personal book. Repeat, repeat, repeat vocabulary; that's how generations past learned to read, and it still works.

Q. *Do I add new books when I think she's getting bored?*
A. No, long before that! I suggest keeping personal books out of reach until a book is mastered; once mastered, it becomes the reader's property. This is motivating and also gives the learner the clear message, "This book is special." Keep introducing new books and materials.

Q. *How do we review the old ones and do both new and old in five minutes twice a day?*
A. Five minutes will become ten minutes and then fifteen… this will naturally happen. As the child's enthusiasm grows, so does his interest and ability to hang in there for longer periods of time. If you sense that your child wants more, definitely keep going. Aim for stopping the session just before he wants to. Temporarily retire old books that haven't quite been mastered, if you like, and bring them out again to review and enjoy again later. Old ones that the child has learned well should now be his permanent possessions!

Q. *I'm having trouble keeping it straight.*
A. Your goal is to make the reading experience fun and enjoyable. Take your cue from the student when determining how long the sessions should be and when new materials are needed to liven things up. Refer to the teaching scaffold in the last chapter as a guide for your teaching.

When Should I Teach?

To repeat my previous advice, for educators, this answer is cut-and-dried for the most part. For parents balancing family and individual needs, I suggest figuring out a plan A, B, and C. If you have only one idea about when would be the best time in a day, afternoon, or evening to do this work and it *doesn't* work at that time, it's too easy to say, "I just can't do this." So do have a backup plan or two figured out. Look for times when neither you nor your child is hungry, tired, or grouchy. If it's just not going to work out on a particular day, skip it that day. Reading should be a wonderful event, shared with enthusiasm. Get to it tomorrow if today is toast.

CHAPTER **10**

Phonics

Unanimous Agreement

As of this writing in 2016, most special education professionals in the United States have thankfully realized that beginning readers with Down syndrome should be taught letter sounds before letter names. Teachers have come to this conclusion as the result of their own experiences and evidence-based practice. It follows logically that learners with autism and other developmental delays would likewise benefit from this revised order of teaching the alphabet. Why is this logical? Because children across the autism spectrum, like children with DS, are typically challenged by limited working memory, short auditory memory, and deficits in auditory processing. In addition, research suggests that individuals with Down syndrome are usually strong visual learners. We want to short-circuit deficiencies and give help in the best way possible.

Here's an example: let's say we're trying to teach the letter *W* to a child. The old school method would teach the name of the letter first. The teacher instructs, "This letter is duh-bhul-yew." Prompting a response, the teacher asks, "So what is this letter?" Often the child answers, "U." "Yew" is the last thing the child heard in her short auditory memory, so that must be the answer, right?

But if we teach the child that the symbol *W* sounds like "wuh," we've given her decoding clout. She now has a tool she can use in her new adventure of reading. Later she'll easily learn that this symbol is *called* duh-bhul-yew. But by then it won't just be an abstract symbol that she has to learn; by then she'll have been using that "wuh" knowledge to effect.

W is not the only renegade in the English alphabet, of course; many letters are in the same club. For example, pronouncing the letter *A* ("ae") sounds nothing like "ah." *B* ("bee") sounds nothing like "buh," etc. In teaching sounds first, we enable decoding skills.

If you want to see a perfect demonstration of difficulty with *W*, and at the same time give yourself a few heartwarming and hilarious moments, go to YouTube and watch two-year-old John David give it a try. (See the references at the back of the book.) I hope that video is available forever for educators and parents to enjoy!

Hold the Phone

At the risk of becoming a target for rotten tomatoes, I believe that, following the mastery of letter sounds, the simplest way to learn to decode is by becoming an experienced reader of whole words that are of very high interest to the reader with Down syndrome. (For those of you who are concerned that I might advise skipping phonics altogether, not to worry; ahead are multiple resources for teaching phonics.) But it should spark curiosity and thoughtful musings when we remember that generations past, mine included, learned to read without phonics. Instead, we had the repetitious help of Dick, Jane, Baby, and Spot. Over and over and over again.

Phonics was out of style and absent from the classroom when I was a child in prehistoric times. Along with my friends, I became a voracious reader, dividing my free time between that and living outdoors on my bike. Even the encroachment of TV into my home (I was eleven) had no impact on reading time, as the few options there included "prize fights" and Ed Sullivan. *The Secret Garden* and *Treasure Island* were incomparably more riveting. Ruefully, I think that while devices and the Internet have opened up vast communication vistas (instantaneous information/research, for starters), it still falls to parents and educators to foster in children a fascination with the world that lies within books.

Looking for Illiteracy Culprits and Solutions

In my own teaching, I augment high-interest books with time spent on games that stress beginning sounds, ending sounds, and spelling games for all that comes in between. That approach is characteristic of "analytic phonics," as opposed to the new "synthetic phonics," which emphasizes identifying phonemes in all positions and then synthesizing or blending them into words.

In my work with children with Down syndrome, I am keenly aware of what confuses and discourages them and what does not. I try to meet the learning needs of the child, and that typically means that I avoid trying to teach complicated phonetic rules that I myself didn't have to struggle to learn.

In our current panic over the decline in reading ability, policymakers are grabbing at phonics (both analytic and synthetic) and hoping that phonics is the solution to the problem. Synthetic phonics, besides putting pressure on educators and expecting children to try to understand in ways that many are not inherently programmed to learn, can destroy the love of reading. There is more on this topic in chapter 1, "Comprehension and Fluency."

I think we would find the "poor reading" culprit if we took even a casual look at the alarming amount of time that school-age children spend on screens today. Video games and similar activities, while they might encourage the development of carpal tunnel syndrome and what has become known to chiropractors as "tech neck," do not develop reading skills. Period. A quick comparison of the daily time students spent on reading for entertainment in 2016 versus time spent on that same activity in 1990 would reveal explanation enough.

For an eye-opener, try doing an Internet search on "influence of electronic media on reading ability." You'll find alarming statistics and studies done with students from around the globe—from Norway to Nigeria and points in between. There are also studies done on students' ability to remember and learn from printed material versus reading that same material on a screen; guess which method scored "significantly better"!

That's why I encourage parents to use time spent on devices as an earned reward (for cooperation, attending, chores done, etc.) and not allow devices to be viewed by either children or parents as entitlements, available to the child most of the time. Our children are not entitled to indiscriminate use of devices! Years ago, parents had the same temptation to use devices as "babysitters;" but in those days, the device was the VHS machine hooked up to the TV. Much easier to control. I know one brilliant mother who, in order to keep her children's brains and bodies active until she returned home from work, took the TV power cord to work with her. No power, no TV. Simple.

Reading for Meaning Leads to Decoding

As children expand their vocabulary through reading *high-interest* books and materials, this leads very naturally to decoding ability. Teachers and parents have observed this happening, and I have as well. My son developed decoding skills effortlessly over three years as I taught him to read through high-interest books, beginning when he was five. By age eight, he had figured out how to decode simply because he was an experienced reader. He is not an anomaly, nor is he at the high end of the Down syndrome spectrum. According to research, a child who progresses through sight word reading to the literacy level of late second grade/early third grade has typically figured it out. He knows how to decode. This is, in fact, the way most of us learned to read.

When my nine-year-old with Down syndrome walked into the kitchen one day, holding one of his favorite "body books" (anatomy for kids) and excitedly talked about "the digestive system and the skeletal system," my jaw dropped. I was his only reading teacher, and I had not taught him those words. I didn't need to. Knowing only letter sounds and names but already having an unusually broad reading experience under his belt, he had simply figured out how to decode. Just like I did, along with countless other baby boomers.

I should not have been surprised—though I was—some years later when Jonathan volunteered information about which the rest of the family was ignorant. We had gone with him to see *The Lion King on Broadway*, and I had gifted him with the uber-program (the expensive one), which he elected to read voraciously at intermission rather than getting a snack. On the way home, as the rest of us were chatting about how awesome the Scar actor was (we hadn't bothered to learn the name of that actor or any other), Jonathan volunteered, "Yes,

Scar was played by Patrick Page. He also played the role of Lumiere in *Beauty and the Beast* on Broadway." There was dead silence in the car as it sank in: he had been *studying* the tiny-print program while the rest of us mindlessly guzzled pop. Talk about motivation and wanting to read for content! It simply works.

It is good to keep in mind that our national/international obsession with phonics, whether synthetic or analytical, is actually a relatively recent phenomenon. The vast majority of us learned to read by sight, by familiarity. And we still use those skills; when we read books, newspapers, magazines, screens, or anything else, we are reading by sight. We decode only when we come across an unfamiliar—and typically complex—word. Then we use our phonemic awareness to work through the pronunciation.

What Would Maria Do?

I'd like to have Maria Montessori weigh in at this point. The United Kingdom's BBC has produced a wonderful documentary series, *Extraordinary Women,* and one of the documentaries is devoted to Maria (see References).

"Does anyone know how Maria Montessori formulated her ingenious teaching methods?" I ask this question in all my workshops. I rarely see a hand go up. And in case your hand isn't in the air yet, I'll give you the answer: she formulated her teaching methods over two years of working exclusively with children with developmental delays. Down syndrome, cerebral palsy, and what today we call autism spectrum disorders—these were among the challenges of her first students.

Fresh out of medical school (she would later go on to earn two additional doctorates, in both psychology and anthropology), Dr. Montessori and a medical colleague were assigned to work at an "insane asylum for adults," as it was called at that time in Italy. Fair enough; that genre of work was within her field. But to her horror, she discovered that *also* housed there were children with developmental delays of all kinds. Society was at a loss as to what to do with these children, so there they were, living dreadful lives in an "asylum."

Determined to remedy the situation, Maria and her colleague opened a school for the children, and for two years taught them daily from 8:00 a.m. to 7:00 p.m. (at which time they returned to the asylum for the night). Over those two years, Maria's brilliant ability to observe and experiment produced such astonishing results that she had the courageous nerve to enter a number of her "special" students in the Italian State Examinations, *without indicating in any way* on paperwork that they were, in the rough terminology of the day, "idiot children."

So what happened? *They all passed the examination*, which focused on reading and writing. Some of them even did better than their typical peers, which caused quite an uproar, and at that point, education the world over began to change under Maria's influence.

So how did she teach these children with special needs to read? As children traced sandpaper letters mounted on wooden slates, they were taught the *sounds* of each. They were given large sandpaper letters to assemble into words, and reading and writing developed naturally. To quote directly from the BBC documentary, "She provided no other instruction, and the children learned to read as if they had taught themselves. This was unheard of."

And in Maria's own written words (translated): "Supposing I said there was a planet without schools or teachers, study was unknown, and yet the inhabitants—doing nothing but living and walking about—came to know all things, to carry in their minds the whole of learning: would you not think I was romancing? Well, just this, which seems so fanciful as to be nothing but the invention of a fertile imagination, is a reality. It is the child's way of learning. This is the path he follows. *He learns everything without knowing he is learning it...*"

I am suggesting that, just as Maria Montessori taught reading to her students with special needs, *there is a way to learn to read without knowing you are learning it.*

How Did You Learn to Read?

This is another question I ask in all my reading workshops. "How did you learn to read? How many of you here learned to read through phonics?" Out of an audience of fifty or so educators and parents, typically one or two hands are raised. Yet everyone present, I assume, reads quite well indeed.

It baffles me that we would require our already-struggling readers with special needs to memorize complicated phonics rules that we ourselves didn't have to grapple with. Why are we doing this? And why are we doing this when there are easier options for reaching the goal of independent reading?

Phonics as it is widely taught today requires auditory discrimination, an excellent auditory memory, and top-notch working memory: the ability to retain and work with a number of different bits of information simultaneously. That complex world of phonics rules—which is particularly overwhelming where the rule-bending language of English is concerned—is beyond many, if not most, of our children with delays.

To quote Glenn Doman, "Reading is a brain function; spelling is a set of rules." And phonics is a set of rules. I doubt that anyone would argue with that.

We read for content. We *all* read only for content. And we all read by sight. Not one of us reading this book is decoding as we go; we know all of these words by familiarity, by sight. That said, some readers of this book will want strategies to help with phonics and decoding, so let's look at some of those tools.

The Engelmann Technique of Decoding

Teach Your Child to Read in 100 Easy Lessons by Siegfried Engelmann, Phyllis Haddox, and Elaine Bruner is a resource worth looking at for developing phonemic awareness. I don't recommend a literal use of it; it was designed for neurotypical learners and would take far longer than a hundred easy lessons for our students to master. But I like the multisensory approach: the child uses a finger to trace the order of phonemes from left to right, matching her vocal expression of the sound to her finger. It's easy to see whether she is actually connecting visual to auditory, or if she is robotically parroting the word. It's a helpful way to teach children to move through sounds and complete a word.

A number of features in the method are useful, so I recommend a closer look—pick and choose your tools from Engelmann's book. Another feature I like: in a word being taught, silent letters are made to look like inferior citizens—they are half the size of the sounded letters and have no "sound dot" underneath the letter. A black dot underneath a letter coaches a child to sound it out; no dot means no sound. In later steps, the dots are dispensed with.

Teaching Beginning Decoding Skills

We want to make this simple; there is no need to complicate the task—either ours or the students'. Children with Down syndrome and other developmental disabilities do not play well with unnecessary complications.

So, I suggest that we simply start work on decoding skills with CVC words (consonant-vowel-consonant) such as *cat, dig, cap, red,* etc. It's a good starting point for teaching about beginning sounds, ending sounds, and eventually—heaven help us—everything that lies in between. If a learner's auditory discrimination and working memory are up to the task, synthetic phonics can help; if not, we want to avoid discouragement at all costs and choose the simpler way. I have seen too many permanently discouraged teens and adults who, based on past experiences in the classroom, have decided that they have zero interest in learning to read. Remember the FOF syndrome: Fear of Failure. FOF closes the door on growth and success. We do all we can to keep the door open.

English is a ridiculously complicated language to decode for reading. In some languages, what you see is what you sound—Italian being one of those languages, which certainly made Maria's job easier. But the English language? How about *thoroughly, daughter, though, whistle,* and *scissors* for starters? Now I ask you, what were our ancestors *thinking* when they developed this visual means of communicating auditory units such as, "Me hungry. Where dinner?" or "Cave dirty. What you do all day?"

Decoding Tools

Decoding English may be a bear, but there are now countless apps that help with the task of learning letter sounds and beginning decoding skills, and a quick online search will give you more than you can possibly use. My favorite for teaching letter sounds is the app "Starfall ABC," an inexpensive but terrific tool in the hands of a parent or educator. At every tap of a finger on a letter, we get the letter *sound,* not the name—though of course the name is introduced at the beginning. This ability to repeatedly tap to get the sound—which the student repeats—can be done ad infinitum; it's a teacher's dream.

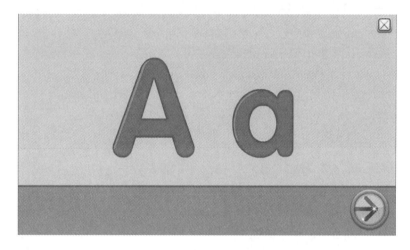

Likewise, a stroll through any Lakeshore Learning Company store, or similar, will offer you a plethora of tools to teach decoding. A trip to Toys R Us will do the same, as will select shopping at "Stuff-Mart" stores. *The best guidance in this arena is to try to match the interests, skills, and learning styles of your student with the app or hands-on gadget.*

One phonics tool I find useful is Lakeshore Learning Company's phonics sets titled "Phonics Magnetic Word

Building Board." Don't search for "Magnetic Word Building Board," on their site (www.lakeshorelearning.com) or you'll get a very different product. The *phonics* sets include the following titles: *3-Letter Words* (CVC words), *Digraphs, Short Vowels, Long Vowels,* and *Blends.* It's fun and hands-on, and the children are the initial directors, as they get to choose magnetic pictures of the words they want to spell. I suggest starting with either the *3-Letter Words* or the *Long Vowels* sets, the easiest for our children to master.

The Magic Pull Card

One tool I keep practically tethered to my hand during teaching sessions is what one parent calls my "magic card." It's a blank white card the size of a business card, and it's particularly useful for learners past the very initial stages of reading.

A new student—I'll call him Liam—came in with his mother; he was reading nicely, at about a second-grade level, but his mother wanted some help with decoding and fluency. She sat directly behind her son during the session and so couldn't see what was happening in front of the child. As Liam read, he did well until he came to longer, unfamiliar words. At those times, I quickly covered all of the word except the beginning syllable, which he could easily read. In effect, I narrowed the field and reduced the task size. Once he had verbalized the initial syllable, I pulled the card away from the rest of the word gradually, and he read it easily, partly using his decoding ability and partly making inferences from the story line.

Afterward, his mother said, "What is that? A *magic* card? Liam stopped reading, you put that card down on the book, and he read the word. *What was happening?*"

We make things easier by reducing the task size and the visual field. With students who have a dual diagnosis such as Down syndrome with autism, I cover all but the one line I am asking the child to read. The rest of her visual field looks like a blank white field. This is very helpful for relaxing the reader and helping her focus. (There is more on working with ASD/autism in chapter 13 on secondary diagnoses.)

Resources for a Lifetime of Teaching Phonics

There are tomes available that can give you more ideas than you can imagine for teaching phonics to our learners with developmental needs. Here are my recommendations:

- *Teaching Reading to Children with Down Syndrome* by Patricia Oelwein (see chapter 10);

- *Try Reading Again: How to Motivate and Teach Older Beginners, Age 10 and Up* by DeAnna Horstmeier (see chapters 5–9), and

- the entire series of *Reading and Writing for Individuals with Down Syndrome* produced by Down Syndrome Education International/USA (dseusa.org).

I particularly like the age-targeted DSEI series, as there are four volumes: *Overview, Infants 0–5 years, Children 5–11 years,* and *Teenagers 11–16 years.* It's easy to target the learner's needs by age, which narrows your focus and increases your effectiveness in teaching.

And as a final resource for learning letter shapes and beginning through advanced handwriting skills, there is nothing better for children with delays than *Handwriting Without Tears* (www.hwtears.com). Though designed for general education, the program works beautifully for our students. It meets all of the guidelines I gave in the beginning chapters of this book: small task size, simplicity, clarity, oversized (hands-on) materials, and repetition...they are all present and glowing in the HWT program.

As you approach the task of teaching your child phonics, it's good to keep in mind this cautionary quote from Patricia Oelwein's book: "Learning to use phonics to decode words is a long, ongoing process, and concepts can become very complex for some children with Down syndrome...When learning words purely by sight, each word is practiced enough times for the learner to immediately recognize the specific combination of symbols as a word...The use of phonics involves learning letter and letter combination sounds and the rules concerning the use of them, then transferring this knowledge to decode words. It involves problem-solving skills in determining which rules apply to what situation. In addition to having difficulty using these concepts, many children with Down syndrome have hearing impairments that make it difficult for them to discriminate sounds."

"A long, ongoing process" is, I believe, the operative concept! And this quotation can certainly be applied to diagnoses other than Down syndrome, diagnoses that mirror the same developmental delays and difficulties that we find in Down syndrome.

Hold the Rebus!

And lastly, here's one "tool" I urge you *not* to use: please don't use any rebuses in your teaching materials. What's a rebus? A rebus is a miniature picture used in place of a word or part of a word, or in proximity to a word (above it or below it). You'll see this crutch used in classroom material and even (gasp) in books in Barnes and Noble. The well-intentioned idea is that somehow this will help an emergent reader to learn the word, wrongly assuming that the child's memory will couple the image and word together. It will not. It will, in fact, delay learning.

Think about what you're asking the brain to do in this instance: one of the right brain's functions is to remember pictures. Some of the left brain's responsibilities are to remember words, details, and process information. Which is easier to look at if you're not yet a fluent reader? The picture, of course. The word doesn't actually create much more than a tiny a neurological ripple; the right brain hemisphere is still engaged with the picture. End of focus on actually learning to read the word!

One thing rebus use *does* do is to create a false impression of reading progress. Take that word away from the rebus and test its recognition in a generalized setting, and the student is likely to have zero recognition. The use of rebuses is counter-productive. Just don't.

Yellow Warning Light: Meet the Need

The bottom line is always to *meet the needs of the child*. Sometimes that will mean avoiding specific training in phonics because it will frustrate a child. Other children will be amenable to some extra help, and others might truly need even more decoding help.

If, because of state requirements or your own convictions, you must teach analytic or synthetic phonics, I recommend that you proceed with wisdom. Teach phonics in a manner that does not either frustrate or discourage the student. Remember, your only goal is to create an enthusiastic and successful reader, one who reads for content; to accomplish that, you must *meet the needs of the child*, teaching her in whatever way she is best able to learn.

Only recently, the decades-old debate over the use of phonics versus the whole language approach to reading has settled into the widely accepted general education practice of "balanced literacy." Balanced literacy combines the use of both whole language and phonics, with components of reading aloud, guided reading, shared reading, and much more. I'm glad to see a more balanced approach to teaching reading, but regardless of which practice is chosen, the bottom line should always be: *meet the needs of the child*. For that, we use our innate powers of observation, intuition, and creativity to discern the most effective path on which to guide each learner.

CHAPTER 11

Comprehension and Fluency

Reading for Meaning

Why do we read? In a perfect world, we read to absorb the content in the material in front of us. Whether it's a book, magazine, computer screen, or the ubiquitous smartphone, we only want to "get it," to understand the content that we're reading. That's it.

But this is not a perfect world. Due to many factors, including state requirements and lack of knowledge of best practice, we typically don't begin our emergent readers on the path of high-interest content, with personal books and modified trade books. Instead, we start them out with rules and low-interest materials not knowledgeably designed to make the job of reading easy for the brain. And then we struggle, the readers struggle, and too often one or the other gives up, thinking the task is unreachable.

Content is king. If a child's initial exposure to reading is based entirely on materials that are of high interest *to that particular child,* comprehension follows like an obedient puppy.

Of course it does. Why else would he be spending time with a book except for the fun of reading about things he loves?

Finding Proof in the Comprehension Pudding

I've received many comments from educators and parents who put this approach to the test and were thrilled with the results: high interest, quick learning, and full cooperation. And to that I'll add my own story of *"reading for meaning leads to comprehension."*

I taught my then-five-year-old son, Jonathan, to read with gigantic homemade personal books (gigantic to accommodate large type.) One book after another, with only occasional pictures placed at the end of the book. He devoured them. Each one increased in difficulty, which he easily absorbed because of his high interest in the content. I did not pepper him with comprehension questions; he obviously knew what he was reading.

When he was nine, he had to be reevaluated—that three-year mandatory evaluation that determines whether he still had Down syndrome, don't you know. Just to be sure it hadn't gone away.

Part of the assessment was a reading test. The evaluator handed him a paper and asked him to read the story aloud. He did. The story was of zero interest to Jonathan: it was about a boy wearing boots who waded into a puddle to rescue his puppy. Jonathan hates boots (or any foot covering), and he is deathly afraid of any animal larger than a flea or smaller than an elephant. This story was not on-topic for him.

The evaluator then asked him a barrage of comprehension questions. "Why did the boy go into the water?" "Why was he wearing boots?" etc. I froze. I had not drilled Jonathan in comprehension! But to my immense relief, he calmly and correctly answered all of her questions.

I was astonished. Then it hit me: from the first moment I had put homemade books and flash cards in front of him, *Jonathan always read for content.* Because he had learned to read from books written about his favorite things in life, he'd gotten the crazy idea that the whole purpose of learning to read words was *so that he could understand what the book said.* What a concept!

No Reading Machines

What we truly want to avoid is the opposite: producing children who are "reading machines." These children can decode flawlessly and race through a reading assignment (typically not stopping for periods or commas) without the slightest understanding of what they just read. How does this happen?

It happens when phonics and decoding are set as the introductory goals of reading. Who or what is to blame? For starters, many state regulations throw roadblocks in the way of natural learning progression, complicated by a general lack of knowledge of how our children with developmental delays can best and most easily learn.

One of my heroes is Great Britain's Children's Laureate of 2007–2008, Michael Rosen. He's the author of *We're Going on a Bear Hunt* and over one hundred other children's books. In 2008, Rosen led a posse of ninety-plus British children's book authors and illustrators who were trying to block the United Kingdom's adoption of "synthetic phonics." Rosen made impassioned pleas to instead *foster the love of reading* by exposure to the wealth of children's books. Instead of imposing rules and regulations, he urged generating interest and skill in reading through a love of children's literature—an experience enthralling, enriching, and mind-expanding. Sadly, he and his team lost, and England adopted synthetic phonics. But he's my hero for trying. If you want to hear him plead his case, just search for "Michael Rosen on phonics" on YouTube (see References at the back of the book).

What Now? We Can't Back Up the Train

But what if this backward effort is already in place? What if the learner operates under the pressurized concept that "reading is all about decoding"? Chances are high that he's lost his love of reading by this time and that reading has become a chore, not a delight. Why should he bother to comprehend material in which he has zero to no interest?

We can swing into action in two critical ways: first, rekindle his love of reading. Second, use comprehension techniques that are effective for that particular child. I'll cover the love of reading first, because frankly, the second action won't do you much good if the first isn't already in place.

1. Rekindle the Fire

Depending on the learner's age, you'll want to initially focus on either personal books or modified books to get the enthusiasm going again—if it was ever present! You're not going to get comprehension on board if you don't have attention on board. That should be obvious, but we tend to forget that in our quest to teach decoding skills. In this book, we've looked at how the brain learns best and how essential it is to poke those neuromodulators into flaming production. Without enthusiasm and attention, comprehension can lie cold and unconscious.

Rekindling has to be both age-appropriate and highly motivating. A six-year-old might need a personal book about his puppy or his favorite TV character; a thirteen-year-old boy who plays percussion in his marching band is going to need a really cool modified book on percussion instruments or marching bands, and so on.

These new personal "hot topic" books or modified on-target trade books will get the fire of enthusiasm and interest sparking again. You can review chapters 4 and 7 on "how to" for both personal and modified books to get this project going.

2. Find Comprehension Techniques That Work

For readers with developmental delays, we can expect comprehension to lag behind several grade levels. This is simply something we anticipate and patiently work with, step by step, knowing that while direct referential comprehension will be relatively easy to develop, inferential comprehension is a significant challenge for most of our learners.

Each student with developmental delays will learn well with specific comprehension techniques; the difficulty lies in finding which ones. For those who want to dive deeper into comprehension techniques past the ones I will give here, I recommend additional reading in the second edition of the tome *Strategies That Work: Teaching Comprehension for Understanding and Engagement,* by Stephanie Harvey and Anne Goudvis. Interestingly, the authors—who wrote this text for teachers of typically developing students—also stress beginning with short, *high-interest* text, just as I have urged throughout this book. If this is best advice for neurotypical students who lag behind in comprehension, how much more so is it for our students?

Here are some basic comprehension strategies:

- *Don't interrupt the reader for the purpose of decoding a word.* Let me explain. If help can be given in the space of a second or two, fine. If you stop the sentence flow for any longer than that, there is little hope for comprehension. The learner, once interrupted, will have forgotten the first part of the sentence, or the gist of the preceding sentence, etc. Working memory is typically limited, and you want the flow of the sentence's concept to be uninterrupted so it makes sense to the reader. You will keep a running record of word errors and tackle that decoding task separately, working out the kinks in a decoding session apart from reading aloud. Reading is about content; stopping the train, getting off and doing a bit of weeding, getting back on the train—that's not going to work in favor of comprehension.

- *Have the student read the sentence aloud twice and then once silently to himself.* Give him a chance to internalize what he's read.

- *Keep the level of reading difficulty quite manageable: 90–95 percent known vocabulary.* We want as much fluency as possible to give comprehension a chance, so we increase difficulty incrementally, erring on the side of caution. Progressing the vocabulary more slowly is better than advancing it too quickly.

- *Begin by color-coding direct reference material to answer "wh" questions.* For learners with Down syndrome and other developmental disabilities, comprehension requiring inference is typically difficult. It will take time and patience to develop. But direct reference is an easier starting position, and I recommend the strategy of color-coding "wh" questions to correspond to answers directly found in the text just read. Here's an example from my "First Grade Bundle" (see www.specialreads.com), which contains comprehension worksheets. The first version is color-coded; the second version gives no coding help and is used once the student begins to understand how to find the referred information. You'll have to use your imagination, as this book is not in color: "Who" is color-coded yellow to match the yellow highlighting of "The puppy," "what" is color-coded green, etc.

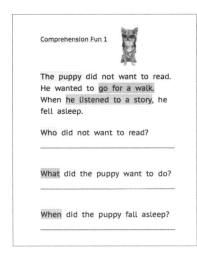

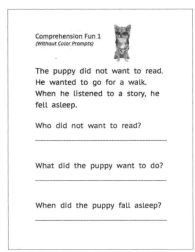

■ *Encourage active reading vs. passive reading to bring home ideas and comprehension.* To quote Harvey and Goudvis, "Teaching reading comprehension is mostly about teaching thinking." Developing active reading techniques can encourage thinking and comprehension. Sticky notes can be used in several ways.

● As the learner is reading a page, use stickies with simple codes such as these: a question mark when a passage is not understood; a star for a favorite passage; "define" if a word needs to be looked up in the dictionary, etc. This is a nice way of moving through a page or pages without laborious discussion. Come back to those sticky notes and tackle each one quite apart from the task of reading.

- Stickies can also be used to sequence the story's action on a separate board. Harvey and Goudvis also recommend the time-honored approach to annotating a book: write in the margins, highlight, dog-ear the pages, make it your own...you get the idea.

- Use two colors of standard sticky notes: one for comprehension questions and one for the child's answers. After the child has read a sentence/paragraph/page (depending on reading ability), you can write a simple comprehension question on a note and stick it on the page. Help the child formulate an answer. Then take the other color of sticky note and write the child's answer on it; stick that on the page. You can work through a book that way, or just a page, depending on the child's ability, and comprehension review later is simplified.

■ *Do a "picture walk" with younger readers.* When picture books are age-appropriate for the learner, consider doing a picture walk through the book first, "reading" the pictures and talking about the story. You can talk about what the pictures might be predicting, getting the child involved and interested. Then begin to read it through. I'll quote Harvey and Goudvis again here: "We can teach readers strategies for thinking by viewing the illustrations as well as through reading." This will also help the child focus when he reads through the book, as the pictures will already be familiar and therefore less distracting.

■ *Pete and repeat.* Having a student read a sentence, paragraph, or page several times in succession not only helps fluency but also increases comprehension. This especially applies to classroom work, where interest is not as high. The first time through a sentence, the emergent reader is typically focused intently on just trying to read the words, period. If fluency and speed are poor, by the time the child gets to the end of a sentence, he can't remember the beginning. This is natural. So have him immediately read the sentence a second and then a third time before asking comprehension questions or moving on to the next sentence or thought. Repetition also applies to an entire book. If a book is a much-loved one, reading it aloud again and again only deepens a child's attachment to the joy of reading—not to mention increasing fluency.

■ *Use the Silly Questions technique.* This tip helps both fluency and comprehension. One of my students—I'll call him Mark—had to read a report aloud for his class and needed practice. The topic was Scottish terriers (interesting to him only because he *has* one). One of the sentences was beyond both Mark's current reading level and his language fluency. *"Scottish Terriers like to hunt raccoons, mice, and rats."* So here's the technique, which worked beautifully:

> Me: "Do Scottish Terriers like to hunt turtles?"
> Mark: "No!"
> Me: "What do they like to hunt?"
> Mark (reading): "Scottish Terriers like to hunt raccoons, mice, and rats."

I continued asking questions I knew would amuse him until he got fluency flowing with that sentence. "Do Scottish Terriers like to hunt bears? Pigs? Elephants?" In the end, his fluency was uncharacteristically terrific. I asked his mom later how the class presentation had gone. She said, "He knocked it out of the park!"

Modifying Classroom Materials for Comprehension

At some point in the future, I hope we will have an information bank containing modified classroom material. That way, parents and aides won't have to reinvent the wheel by laboring over the very same materials that someone, somewhere, sometime previously modified. But at the moment, we are faced with a do-it-yourself modification of classroom material when we're working on reading comprehension—or homework in general.

The visual guidelines for modifying are the same as those I've described in previous chapters: you have to be sure you're "designing for the brain" by using large type, extra spacing between words, lots of white space, text blocks that are not too long, etc. But you also need some general guidelines so that you can get the job done and help the child learn the core information.

A good starting point is to ask the classroom teacher what she or he considers to be the "minimum learning outcome" of any particular assignment. Perhaps there might be three or four major points of information that are crucial to understand in a passage from a workbook. The teacher can determine what those points are, and the parent or aide can then create a comprehension or homework sheet that can communicate that information clearly.

The modification *must* match the child's cognitive ability. This should be obvious, but sometimes in the complexity of the classroom, this can get overlooked. The homework should be achievable. Success should be attainable.

Step 1: Rewrite the reading passage in a concise, simplified version.

Step 2: Formulate a question for each one of the minimum learning outcome points.

Step 3: Assist the child in finding the answers to those questions in the passage you've rewritten.

Step 4: If you're the parent, then of course send in that modified homework to the teacher. It should be previously arranged that this modification should not only be accepted by the educator but applauded!

I realize that this approach is labor intensive and that some parents simply won't have the time to do it; but for children in inclusive classrooms, this modification will make it possible for them to keep pace with the essential material being taught. In other words, it will make it possible for them to be more truly included.

Fluency = Comprehension Precursor

By fluency in reading, I mean the ability to read phrases and sentences smoothly and quickly. We're not going to achieve higher comprehension levels without fluency first being in place. That's simply a fact. To quote Diane Murphy, a national fluency trainer, "Fluency is really the bridge between decoding and comprehension." Simply put, if you interrupt fluency, you derail comprehension.

We know that most students with Down syndrome or other developmental disabilities have a shorter working memory capacity than we might wish for, yet the better the fluency, the more information can be retained in a shorter period of time. We can maximize the student's working memory space—and therefore comprehension—by upping the fluency speed.

- **Fluency Rule # 1: Don't Interrupt.** I've covered this earlier in this chapter, but it bears repeating. If you interrupt with decoding work or comprehension questions, you sabotage both fluency *and* comprehension. So while the student reads aloud, you will keep running records of the difficult/missed words and work on those in a separate session. During the reading session itself, if the student hesitates, give him whatever prompt is needed to keep fluency going: give him a prompt of the first letter sound or the first syllable or even the word itself as needed. As I explained in describing the use of the "magic pull card," if you use that technique, keep it to one or two seconds. Keep the flow going and do the necessary decoding work later in a separate session.

- **Fluency Rule #2: Repeat.** Depending on the skill level of the student, repetition of a sentence, several sentences, or a paragraph three times gives fluency a boost. I've timed some of my students, and reading time can be cut nearly in half by the third repetition. Each time they read the passage, of course, their comprehension also moves up a notch. Repetition is king. Repetition is king. Repetition is king.

- **Fluency Rule #3: Model.** The teacher can model fluency by reading the student's passage after his first read-through. He needs to *hear* how it can flow. So somewhere in that three-time repetition, the teacher can model that same passage for him. Another thing I do with students that helps support fluency is to read a passage *with him* somewhere in that repetition sequence. "Wind beneath my wings" comes to mind whenever I apply this strategy. The student feels less pressure to perform and feels your speed-support underneath him. Will he usually be saying each word slightly after you do? Yes, and that's fine when used as an early strategy. He's learning how fluency *feels*.

Elements of fluency include not just speed and accuracy, but other qualities much harder for students with Down syndrome and other developmental challenges to achieve: expression, phrasing, and intonation.

This is particularly difficult for students who innately ignore punctuation when reading. It almost seems that they interpret commas and periods to be a sign for "keep going; don't stop!" So a first step in acquiring these "extra" elements of fluency would be red-flagging punctuation. On "owned" materials that can be modified permanently, you might use a green or blue highlighter to highlight punctuation wherever it occurs. Yellow is not obvious enough, but green and blue are friendly and not too obtrusive. The result, hearing a child read with expression, is enormously rewarding. I give tremendous praise to students who actually read a question with vocal intonation rising at the end of the sentence. It's beautiful to hear, and reinforces proof that they have understood what they've read.

In Summary

One of my blog readers, a retired classroom and Reading Recovery teacher (whose name I regrettably did not record), commented: "I have said for many, many years that children who learn to read for meaning in the beginning will be life-long readers and will have no problem with comprehension! Though it takes extra time to create self-interest books, it is well worth the effort...The more personal reading and writing becomes, the more your child will grow in literacy skills!"

I agree, absolutely.

Wouldn't you expect that if an emergent reader is reading a personal book about the games he and his adored big brother play together, he would totally understand everything he's reading and could answer any question about the text? *Make reading personal, and comprehension will soar.*

CHAPTER **12**

Errorless Testing and Fear of Failure

No-Pressure Testing

In line with our intention to encourage, not discourage, learners—and to avoid what I call FOF, or Fear of Failure syndrome, I suggest that we follow the lead of Patricia Oelwein. In her book, *Teaching Reading to Children with Down Syndrome*, Oelwein details the method she uses to ensure that children with Down syndrome avoid failure when learning to sight read. It is an approach involving—in order of increasing difficulty—matching, selecting, and naming written words.

But what is FOF syndrome? It's an anecdotal acronym, of course, not an official diagnosis. But we have all seen it in some form or another when we teach: all humans shrink from failure, but our children perhaps have a greater sensitivity to failure than most—they must face its possibility continually. If they think a task is beyond them, they often refuse to cooperate rather than fail at it. FOF syndrome can take many forms: the learner may shut down, withdraw, act out, or literally turn away. A child with good verbal skills may express that fear by saying, "*I can't! No! It's too hard!*"

Avoiding Failure

To avoid failure and the fear of failure, we must pay attention to a few key points:

1. We consider **task size** as all-important: the task must be small enough and manageable enough for the child to succeed. If it's not, we break the task into even smaller units until it matches the learner's ability—until we see that it's *not* "too hard."

2. We **give prompts** *quickly*. We don't wait for the student to fail. We give either verbal or visual prompts, always encouraging, never with the hidden message, "No, that's wrong."

3. We follow the **fail-safe order** of "match-select-name." When necessary, we present fewer options for the child to choose from. For example, when having the student select or match words, we can use a field of two, three, four, or more words, depending on her skill level.

4. Keep in mind that **any word** we're testing **should already have been flashed** many, many times, used in personal books, etc. These should be words that have already been taught repeatedly, and now we're at the point of wanting to test that knowledge.

Matching

When a student seems to know the words you've been teaching her, you need to determine whether she has simply memorized the story or can actually recognize the word in isolation. We begin the assessment with matching games.

Matching always requires two sets of the words you're working with. You can use duplicates of the flash cards you've used for teaching, or you can create slightly smaller cards. The simplest solution is to use lotto or matching games (see chapter 14 for directions) for this preliminary testing strategy, since your materials are already on hand in the form of a word board and matching word cards.

Chapter 14 describes how to make lotto games of six-words-up and six-pictures-up in detail. Here, I'll only be referring to the *method* of using that word board and its matching cards for testing at the "matching" level. With a lotto board, it's simple to cover words so that the child can match to a field of either two, three, four, or six cards. For example:

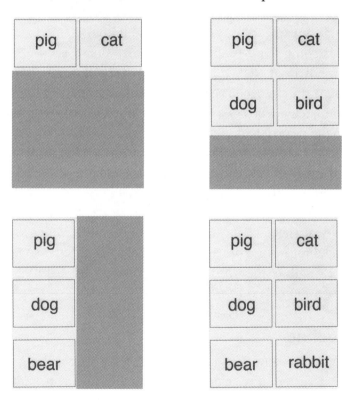

As explained in chapter 14, when you're using any lotto game, you will work with two picture sheets and two word sheets and will cut the duplicate sheets into individual words or pictures.

The simple strategy: As you hand the child one word card, you name the card yourself and ask her to find that same word on the visual field you've prepared. If she hesitates, give verbal or physical prompts quickly to avoid fear of failure kicking in. For example, you might emphasize the beginning sound by saying, for example, "*sssss.*" Or if there is still no sign of recognition, you might tap the correct word on the board. You want to let the learner know that *she can do it*, so move quickly through any uncertainty or apparent failure.

Matching word flashcards to a word board is an activity that lends itself well to breaking down the task into smaller units. As the child gains confidence and experience in her ability to match a word to a field of two, it's much easier to move on to the next step of difficulty.

So if a child correctly matches a word to that same word out of a field of two, three, or more, does that mean she knows the word solidly and can generalize that knowledge? In other words, can she recognize that word anywhere she might see it?

No, not necessarily. In the beginning, children are going to be matching a word based on the initial letter or letter sound—or the length of the word. That's not reading yet, but it's a first step of awareness.

Selecting

After the child seems comfortable with the matching task, you can move on to selecting. Selecting is done with individual word cards instead of a word board, but the technique of using a small task size is done just as in the illustration for "matching."

The simple strategy is this: say a word aloud and then ask her to select that word from a field of two cards initially, then three, four, etc.

Naming

The most difficult task in the lineup of testing strategies—naming a word shown without any prompts from the teacher—comes as the final test of recognizing the words. Simply hold up a card and ask the child to name it. As with the first two testing strategies, if she seems uncertain, quickly use a prompt to encourage her success: in this case, it would be with a verbal prompt, such as sounding out the initial letter sound.

If the child is nonverbal, her response options are these: signing, consistent verbal approximation, or selecting a picture (out of a field of multiple pictures) that corresponds to the word's meaning.

Until the reader has solidly learned the words, continue to show them by Fast Flashing and use them in personal books and materials.

Generalizing

I would like to suggest one more step as a follow-up to the matching-selecting-naming testing techniques. Often a child is able to name a familiar card without prompts but can't read it in a generalized setting. We need for her to be able to recognize that word anywhere, anytime, in any setting.

I typically work on this problem one of two ways. First, I rewrite a page or pages of previously studied material in new ways, always including the child or her family, pets, etc., in the new rewrite. That keeps the interest high, but the order of words is unexpected. Or I might create completely different material using the same core vocabulary with additional words not included in the original material. You can quickly print these little stories by hand with markers (this simulates large type), or if you have a bit more time, type them on a computer using double-spacing and a large sans serif font size.

These "personal pages" are a regular part of my teaching strategy; I create them during the teaching session based on what the student is interested in that day, and I send one or several of these handwritten (large print) sheets home to be practiced that week. Just as with personal books, all topics are welcomed. For example, one student didn't like the beard her dad was experimenting with wearing. So her "personal page" that week included the sentence, "I do not like beards! Beards are crazy." (The word choice was hers.) Did this motivate her to generalize? You bet.

Rewriting does a beautiful job of sabotaging the "memorizing skill" many students with Down syndrome or other developmental disabilities possess. Many of our children, if not most, have a marked ability to memorize text quickly. Your student can use this ability to pull the wool over your eyes unless you rewrite to help her develop the ability to generalize.

CHAPTER

13

Teaching Learners with Autism or Apraxia of Speech

Undiagnosed Secondary Conditions

Autism spectrum disorder (ASD) and childhood apraxia of speech (CAS or apraxia) may be the primary and only diagnosis that a child has. But I have also observed that these are the two most commonly undiagnosed conditions that I see in conjunction with Down syndrome. When they do occur with Down syndrome, the DS typically camouflages the secondary diagnosis, to the detriment of the child and parents. If any secondary—or even tertiary—conditions remain unidentified, the child will not get the specific therapies and treatments that we know are most effective to treat these disorders, and a lifetime of difficulty typically results.

When concerned parents suspect that "something else is going on here" and bring the child in for an evaluation, too often the medical opinion is this: "It's just Down syndrome. We expect speech and cognitive delays, as well as behavioral problems." Frequently the parents are dismissed as being overly fretful.

Nonsense. If a child actually has other diagnoses, his parents and teachers need to know this, and they need to know it as soon as possible so the child can get intervention and the correct services. This tendency to overlook or dismiss a possible additional diagnosis is termed *diagnostic overshadowing,* and we'll take a closer look at that in the section on autism.

Down syndrome is not autism, and Down syndrome is not apraxia. What I call "Plain Vanilla Down Syndrome" does not look like either condition, nor does it look like my son's additional diagnoses of severe attention-deficit hyperactivity disorder (ADHD) and oppositional defiant disorder (ODD).

When my son's behavior escalated into the "red zone" by age seven, I was immensely grateful that Dr. Bonnie Patterson was on board at the Down syndrome clinic at Children's Hospital in our home city of Cincinnati. Dr. Patterson is a renowned expert in the field of DS, and she clearly knew the difference between DS and ADHD. She diagnosed a secondary—and then tertiary—condition so that we could focus on what we were *actually* dealing with. It was not "just Down syndrome." We needed much more help, as do many parents who struggle without knowing the accurate diagnoses of their child.

Childhood Apraxia of Speech

The speech and articulation challenges that we expect to see with Down syndrome or autism are a far cry from the struggles of a child who is somewhere on the CAS spectrum. I have had an unusually high percentage of reading students with the dual diagnosis of DS/CAS, and I can affirm that these two diagnoses are in no way alike.

What is CAS? Here is the definition straight from the American Speech-Language-Hearing Association:

Childhood apraxia of speech (CAS) is a motor speech disorder. Children with CAS have problems saying sounds, syllables, and words. This is not because of muscle weakness or paralysis. The brain has problems planning to move the body parts (e.g., lips, jaw, tongue) needed for speech. The child knows what he or she wants to say, but his/her brain has difficulty coordinating the muscle movements necessary to say those words.

CAS is a brain coordination problem. It is not a developmental problem but a medical condition. The key words I want to highlight in this definition are these: ***"the child knows what he or she wants to say."*** Absolutely. But he can't get those thoughts out through speech. It must be immensely frustrating, and it is no wonder that these children often act out as a result.

Here is a simple example of the difference between a child whose speech is delayed because of Down syndrome alone and one who has the dual diagnosis of Down syndrome and CAS. The child who just has DS might say "Da" or "Dada" when trying to pronounce the word *Daddy*. The child with DS/CAS might be lucky to even verbalize "eee," latching on to the final and easiest sound to produce (i.e., the sound that requires the least amount of muscular coordination). If the child has DS/CAS, most frequently the sound he can produce consistently for a word may not sound similar at all to the actual word. But if he uses that sound consistently for that particular word, those who work with him get to know his meaning.

There are several quicksand traps to be aware of if your child has CAS. No matter where on that spectrum the child might be, from severe to mild, there are four problems parents are likely to encounter:

1. **Unqualified evaluation.** Have your child evaluated by a *qualified* speech-language pathologist (SLP) or a developmental pediatrician who is knowledgeable about both CAS and Down syndrome and sees a clear distinction between the two. Why? Because unless the evaluator has this specialized knowledge, CAS will not be identified, and your child's evaluation form will identify the problem with the words *developmental delay* rather than *CAS*. CAS is a medical diagnosis and entitles the child to get services such as CAS-specific speech therapy (versus "group" speech therapy offered at school, which is essentially a language class). "Developmental delay" is *not* a medical diagnosis and will not merit the needed services. This is essential to know. Again, quoting from the ASLHA website: *"It is important to have your child evaluated by a speech-language pathologist (SLP) who has knowledge of CAS to rule out other causes of speech problems."*

2. **Misinformation.** Parents might be told that, as long as the child is receiving speech therapy at the school or privately, this will address the child's need. Not! CAS therapy sessions are designed differently than typical speech therapies. The two are not equal. In a private speech therapy session, a child might be taught "b" as the "buh" sound with many words (*ball, baby, bat, balloon,* etc.). But if the child has apraxia and is being given therapy specific to CAS, the "buh" sound might be taught with only one or two words beginning with

"b." Those two simple words might be repeated count-less times to help the child actually begin to produce the "buh" sound. The word *baby* might be chosen as an exercise over the word *bat,* for instance, as *bat* would also require an entirely different brain-motor coordi-nation to produce the ending "t."

3. **Low expectations in the classroom.** Because the child is nonverbal and unable to express thoughts and demonstrate all of his abilities, the great temptation for educators, therapists, etc., is to assume low cognitive skills. Contrary to this expectation, I have found that my students with DS/CAS tend to be cognitively on the high end of the scale, not the low end. But how can they express their needs, wants, or thoughts? This is where correct therapies and the use of AAC devices (augmentative and alternative communica-tion devices) can save the day. There are AAC apps for iPads, which children with CAS can use beautifully; a quick online search will turn up many. One of the top recommended apps to enable communication in chil-dren who are nonverbal is Proloquo2go, and you can find it easily online.

4. **School says no to speech therapy, no to signing.** A child who is nonverbal may be denied speech therapy by the school because "he has no language." The same child may be denied the opportunity to learn sign lan-guage—by the same school!—because "we want him to learn how to speak." I am not making this utterly crazy-making situation up; I have had students in this predicament. Get legal help, or, less expensively, get an accurate diagnosis of CAS, if that is indeed what your child has.

Autism Spectrum Disorder

Autism by itself is now typically diagnosed early and well. When it is coupled with Down syndrome, the storyline is not as encouraging: identification is typically difficult and late. According to current statistics, an estimated 7 to 10 percent of children with Down syndrome are likely to have a dual diagnosis of Down syndrome and autism. But as a secondary diagnosis, ASD is difficult for physicians to spot.

Why is this difficult? For one reason, DS and autism share a number of crossover characteristics: delayed speech and language skills, difficulties with social skills, self-stimulation ("stimming" or deliberately making movements or sounds that seem to have no useful purpose), and restricted interests (but we take good advantage of this last one when we create personal books!)

The overlap of Down syndrome and autism is, however, quite easy for a specialist to observe. If you are lucky enough to have such a qualified developmental pediatrician in your city, fantastic. If not, a highly recommended source I've learned of from parents who have gone there is the Anna and John J. Sie Center for Down Syndrome at Children's Hospital in Colorado. The medical director at the center is Dr. Francis Hickey, eminently qualified not only medically, but also because he has a teenage son with both Down syndrome and autism.

Quoting from the University of Colorado's *Medicine Today* (see References), "Dr. Hickey learned early on that his fellow physicians tended to engage in 'diagnostic overshadowing'— overlooking associated conditions like sleep apnea or hypothyroidism and autism, writing them off as simply 'due to Down syndrome.'" In Dr. Hickey's words, "I always say 'listen to the parents.' If they have concerns and you don't address them, you may miss something. Autism is a perfect example."

For parents and educators who want to look more deeply into this dual diagnosis, I recommend *When Down Syndrome and Autism Intersect: A Guide to DS-ASD for Parents and Professionals* by Margaret Froehlke and Janet Zaborek.

Teaching Learners with DS-ASD

This next point is important. If your child has the dual diagnosis of DS-ASD, do you teach to the Down syndrome, or do you teach to the autism? Autism, hands down. Autism trumps Down syndrome. Your major focus at this point is teaching to the challenges of autism, not Down syndrome, beginning with the difficult task of engaging the child's awareness, interest, and attention in the first place—and then keeping it. I have urged this view of "teach to the autism diagnosis" in my workshops for years, speaking only from experience and not clinical research, so I was glad to hear my view affirmed at a recent workshop. One mother who had taken her son (who has DS-ASD) to see Dr. Hickey in Colorado said, "That's just what Dr. Hickey told me. You have to teach to the autism."

So how do we "teach to the autism"? My first suggestion is to get an ABA behaviorist on board. Very simply explained, ABA, or applied behavior analysis, is the current go-to intervention for children struggling with behavioral challenges in general, and autism in particular. The ABA specialist will typically observe the child in various settings—home, school, therapies, etc., and decide on an approach that all those involved with the child will use to modify behavior and make everyone's life easier, including the child's. It's not always easy to find a good match with the child; a friend of mine whose son has the DS/ASD diagnosis ran quickly through two behaviorists before she found the third, a specialist who changed her son's life—and her family's—in amazing ways. Today, you would not even know from her son's behavior that he has a dual diagnosis.

"If you've met one person with autism, you've met one person with autism." You've probably heard this said, and the truth of that statement makes teaching a child with autism challenging. What works with one child with autism will not necessarily work for another. This is also true across the spectrum of developmental disabilities, isn't it? But as far as technical tips in teaching learners with autism or DS/ASD, I have found several things to be very helpful:

1. **Dim the lights and ditch the fluorescent bulbs.** Research has found that fluorescent bulbs are harmful in more ways than one, especially in the classroom. It's worthy of an Internet search. I have found that soft, dim incandescent lighting is calming and soothing to learners when autism is involved (and even when it's not). I avoid using LED bulbs (tempting because they last forever) because their predominant light is in the blue range of the spectrum, which stimulates rather than soothes. Incandescent lighting tends toward a warmer yellow. There is another significant reason to dim the lights in the teaching area: it helps dim the distracting visual details in the immediate environment. A child with autism may be drawn inexplicably to focus on some tiny detail in his surroundings that has nothing to do with the task in front of him. Creating a dimmer, more muted visual environment helps to both increase focus and soothe agitation.

2. **Use brain music softly in the background.** This is also soothing and helps with focus. Play the music so softly that the student doesn't notice it; the brain notices, and that's all we want. We don't want the student distracted.

(Review the section on brain music in chapter 6, "Teaching to the Brain.")

3. **Let the learner use a flashlight pen to move from word to word.** This helps with focus, puts the child in charge (always a plus), and of course shines the spotlight on what you're asking him to read.

4. **Cover all text except the line the child is reading.** I use two white laminated sheets to cover the text both above and below the line of type the student is reading. For children with autism who notice small visual distractions, this is a big help.

5. **Keep the type large.** Even for a more advanced reader, this helps prevent brain fatigue; it's simply easier to read.

6. **Know when to stop.** You can actually observe that brain fatigue happening right before your eyes. Perhaps two pages ago, the student was rocking right along, reading well. Now he's faltering, and you can tell that he'll crash if you don't take a break. Here is where some kinesthetic activity can be the perfect solution. (My students' favorite is to turn the lights off and toss a "sparkly" (LED) ball. Give the brain a chance to recover and regroup.

Teaching and Testing Nonverbal Readers

Teaching: We teach nonverbal learners virtually the same way as we teach verbal learners. When requiring a nonverbal student to "read" along with us, we can ask him to use signs or give verbal approximations, as long as those approximations are consistent to the child and the specific word. Make sure the student is using a pointer to keep on target as you are reading the text aloud.

Testing: But of course, we need to test nonverbal students quite differently. There are several effective methods and tools we can use not only to test but also to prove reading ability to school staff and others who may not know sign language, or for whom the child may not be willing to perform on demand. To test reading ability for a child who is nonverbal, we have the options to sign, give verbal approximations, use an ACC device/software, build sentences with tabletop cards, and use other tools such as lotto or matching games.

1. **Use lotto/matching games.** Lotto games can be used to prove reading ability even if the child has no verbal ability whatsoever. You'll read about the seven levels of difficulty in teaching with lotto games in the next chapter, "Teaching Materials." I have found lottos uniquely satisfying to students who are nonverbal; in some cases, it's the very first time they have been able to *show* anyone that they can read! No verbal ability is required to prove knowledge when matching words to pictures or pictures to words. Using the lotto game, we can completely bypass the need for speech. (Look ahead to Chapter 14 for more details on how to use reading lottos.)

2. **Use sentence builders.** This requires more work on the part of the teacher, since all words need to be written *neatly* (or typed) on cards small enough to fit together on a wooden sentence strip (see illustration). The cards necessary to build a sentence are arranged randomly on the table in front of a slotted sentence board. As we coach the child with each word needed to build the sentence, the child chooses from among the words and

builds the sentence. This can also be done without a wooden sentence builder: I sometimes use a long, colored strip of stiff paper and have the child simply place the cards in order on a strip of red paper—or any color that contrasts with the desk surface (see illustration).

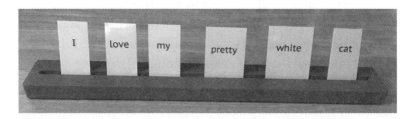

3. **Signing.** Depending on how well the child and the educator use sign language, we can have the child sign the words he's reading. Two problems exist with this method. First, few special educators are fluent in sign language, whether ASL (American Sign Language) or SEE (Signing Exact English.) The second and

significant problem is that children with developmental delays are often quite vague in their signing. It seems to me that they each put their own creative spin on the signs, making it challenging for anyone but their mom and dad to understand what they're communicating. But teaching the student to sign is certainly worth pursuing. Anecdotal recommendations from parents put *Signing Time* (www.signingtime.com) at the top of the preferred list for teaching signing.

4. **Verbal approximations.** I accept any *consistent* vocal approximation as real reading. As long as the learner uses the same sound each time he reads a specific word aloud, I'm content that he is actually reading. Anyone working with that child on a regular basis is going to become familiar with his vocabulary of "substitute sounds" and can encourage and celebrate his success.

Proving: In addition to those testing tips, here are two suggestions you can use to *prove* reading capability to evaluators, educators, or anyone for whom the child may not want to "perform." First, you can create videos of the child reading in any one of the four ways listed above. However, you need to go one step further if you're using signing or verbal approximations as your proof:

1. First take a video of the child signing *his* version of each word that he will later sign when reading a book or whatever material has been chosen. In the video, you will ask the child for each sign that will be used in the book. For example, say, "Sign *cat* for me" and record the child's response. Similarly, you can tape the child's verbal approximation for each word that will be read, if necessary, although the approximation may be

close enough to be recognizable as the word. If that's the case, it's not necessary to make a separate video recording the child's sound for each written word.

2. Then film a second video of the child actually reading the book by the method chosen: either signing or consistently approximating the text verbally.

AAC Proof of Comprehension

Augmentative and adaptive communication devices and iPads loaded with software such as Proloquo2go can be used when programmed with images or text answers to comprehension questions. When the learner who is nonverbal has silently read a passage, the educator can ask comprehension questions, which the child then answers by touching the appropriate word(s) or images already programmed into the app. If this modality works well with the child's learning style, it can be a good option.

The reward of watching the triumph of a child who has just *proved* his ability to read, although he can't speak, is worth whatever it takes to give him that chance.

14

Materials for Teaching Reading

Three Categories of Materials

You essentially have a choice of three categories of materials for teaching reading:

1. those you make yourself (personal books) or modify yourself (trade books and classroom materials)

2. published materials that have been designed for children with developmental delays such as Down syndrome, ASD, etc.

3. published materials designed for neurotypical learners that may, in fact, also work well for learners with delays.

1. DIY Materials

These include *personal books, modified trade books*, and *modified classroom materials*.

We've covered personal books and modified trade books in detail. To modify classroom materials to fit the learning styles and needs of students, you follow the same rules as I've outlined for personal and modified books, with some differences. Obviously, for children in a fully included classroom, we also need to modify general education material so our learners can keep pace with the core information taught in the classroom.

In Chapter 11, "Comprehension and Fluency," I talked about "minimum learning outcomes" and how to modify classroom material to help comprehension. Here I'll repeat the basic guidelines:

- It's essential to modify classroom materials so that they are clearer, simpler, use larger print, and focus on just a very few "minimum learning outcomes" (MLO), the essential points that a child needs to understand from a lesson.

- Ask your child's teacher what the MLOs are for any assignment.

- Rewrite pertinent text at your child's reading level.

- Write comprehension questions that can be answered referentially (the child can literally find the answer by referring back to the text you've rewritten.)

Our goals for personal, trade, and classroom materials are all the same: reading success based on high-interest materials and a brain-friendly design for easy access and retention. For a refresher on the details of "how to," refer to chapters 4 and 7, "Personal Books" and "Modifying Trade Books."

Lotto Games

The one addition to DIY materials I'll discuss here is homemade lotto (matching) games. These can be designed to teach child-specific words: names of family members, pets, favorite foods, etc. I recommend using lotto boards for all emergent readers, *regardless of age level*. These work across the board, no pun intended. This is a favorite tool for both emergent and nonverbal readers, and I have created many sets for my students. I encourage you to create sets like the one below, beginning with pictures and names of family members, etc.—the circle of familiarity that is closest to the student, whatever that might be.

There are no restrictions on topics, as I mentioned in the section on creating personal books: anything goes. For example, if a student with autism has a favorite stimming object or two (objects she uses for self-stimulating, repetitive motion), it is fair game to include them in a lotto. Make the game real and relatable for your child. As with personal books, your primary focus is to engage your child and get her truly interested in reading.

You can create your lotto boards using any software that allows you to create columns; Microsoft Office is a common one to use. For an emergent reader just starting out, you can create a board with four rectangles (two columns of two rectangles each). Later, you can progress to a design of six (two columns of three rectangles). I don't recommend more rectangles than that, since many learners with Down syndrome or other developmental disabilities have five or so memory channels. That means they can hold five or six bits of information comfortably in working memory. If you exceed six rectangles, it tends to be visually confusing.

To make a lotto game, first create two boards with four (or six rectangles). One will be the picture board, and one will be the word board. Drag and drop pictures into the rectangles on the picture board. In the word board document, type the words that correspond to the pictures in the largest font you can manage with the space limitations you have. Use a consistent font size; don't vary the font size from rectangle to rectangle.

Scramble the order of the words on the word board so that they don't match the order of the pictures on the picture board. In other words, avoid putting words in the same board-position as on the picture board. Some of our learners are pros at memorizing picture positions, allowing them to fake reading ability. And don't forget to make large red-letter flash cards for the words on the lotto board.

Once you design your word board and picture board documents, print two copies of each. Laminate all 4 sheets. Then cut the duplicate sheets into cards. (See illustration above of the "pig" lotto set.) Now you're ready to teach.

How to Use Lotto or Matching Games

There are actually seven different levels of difficulty that you can use for a student, depending on his or her level of ability. As always, with whatever materials you are teaching, use method of "sandwiching" the game/book/activity between showings of the core words with the Fast Flash method.

Fast Flash the large red-letter flash cards you've made

1. Match picture to picture
2. Match word to word, with prompts
3. Match word to picture, with prompts
4. Match picture to word, with prompts
5. Match word to word (no prompts)
6. Word to picture (no prompts)
7. Match picture to word (no prompts)

Fast Flash the large red-letter flash cards you've made!

1. Match picture to picture.

As with all reading materials, you will want to Fast Flash the words first, using the "Sandwich Style" teaching model: Flash-Read-Flash.

Two tips:

1. Make the type in these lotto games as large as you can. I have never found published lotto or matching sets with large enough type. I realize, though, that not everyone has the time to create these from scratch, so I've recommended a resource in the "published materials" section at the end of this chapter.

2. When you are designing your boards in Office or whatever software you like to use, remember to place the words in a completely different order than the pictures. I mentioned this earlier, but it bears repeating! Don't simply reverse the columns from left to right, but scramble the positions of the pictures versus the positions of the words. Our children are brilliant position-memorizers for pictures. Once they've seen that a picture of a burger, for example, is in the upper-right corner, then—if you've made the mistake of putting the word "burger" also in the upper-right corner—they will automatically place the picture of the burger in the correct position on the word board even if they're not yet able to read the word. So let's not enable our smart little pretenders!

2. Published Materials for Developmental Delays

As I mentioned, there is a plethora of teaching materials, programs, and apps that you can find on the Internet. The list of materials in this section is not meant to be an exhaustive list. What I offer here are simply a few that I consider among the best.

Birth to Three Years

Love and Learning

Created by Joe and Susan Kotlinski and used by many parents of very young children with special learning needs (birth to three), the Love and Learning reading kits were a favorite of families with children with Down syndrome. In their original hard-copy format, they are no longer available at this time. However, save the URL for the future (http://www.love-andlearning.com), as the company is now developing android apps that will build on the high-focus format the kits have always used. On their site, the Kotlinskis write: "After 30 years of working with families and providing ready-made learning materials, we are no longer able to have the learning kits available for purchase. We will, however, eventually provide instructions for making your own materials. We will be focusing on Android apps that will incorporate the unique features of our technique."

In the meantime, I recommend this link for accessing the essentials of Learning Kit #1: http://loveandlearning.com/kit1. html. This link includes directions to YouTube videos, a free PDF download, and a link to the android e-book app for Kit #1.

When Love and Learning was just getting started thirty years ago, I used that first kit to teach my son Jonathan (DS) the alphabet. He learned all letter sounds and names in less than two months.

How did this happen so quickly? On the TV screen, each letter—shown singly—was huge; depending on your screen, a letter could be many inches high. My five-year-old son was entranced. It was also his *first* screen watching of each day; his TV watching was almost nonexistent, and his DVD time (okay, VHS time—this was in ancient times) had to be earned by completing chores. So his brain was fairly uncluttered and free of "device influence."

Strengths of the *Love and Learning* program included *large type* (where have you heard this before?); an uncluttered design, clear in its teaching; and—whether the Kotlinskis knew it or not—a video design that played right into right-brain learning. After the important information was given (letter shape and sound), a short video of an activity with that object was viewed with delightful music. Enter: the relaxation and engagement of the right-brain hemisphere, responsible for long-term memory storage!

A word of advice about showing your child any instructional video (and hopefully it's clear, with large type): I recommend that this type of material be the *first* viewing of the day on *any* device. We want to use teaching DVDs or apps that are simple and lack the overstimulation of today's apps/TV/games. The brain will be more receptive and retentive if it hasn't been subjected to split-second stimulation. Let this information go into a more receptive brain; let it be viewed first.

Toddlers and Beyond

See and Learn

Another resource I recommend is Down Syndrome Education International (https://www.dseinternational.org/en-us/). For over thirty years, DSEI has been the global leader in developmental and educational research for children with Down syndrome. As far as I am concerned, the organization is the gold standard and the top resource for keeping the world abreast of understanding how children with Down syndrome learn best. For a number of years, the DSEI had its own classroom clinic, an awesome testing ground for the research and development of its many publications. Out of that classroom setting came a number of programs, including the *See and Learn* program, which now includes iPad apps and app bundles (http://tinyurl.com/DSEIapps).

Currently, the *See and Learn* program supports development of skills in children with Down syndrome in three areas: speech, language and reading, and numbers (Numicon is recommended). The DSEI language and reading program includes activities designed to help young children with Down syndrome learn to speak, and introduces them to letter sounds and beginning sight words. For older children, DSEI offers the Reading and Language Intervention (RLI) program, a system designed to be used in a pull-out setting; it's an evidence-based method that provides individualized language and reading activities geared to children with DS ages five to eleven.

See and Learn First Word Pictures is one place to start and to help children identify objects. DSEI's *See and Learn* program includes many kits; if you follow that link online, you'll see them all.

One of my favorite resources for information on many aspects of living, working with, and teaching individuals with Down syndrome is the DSEI's *iiSeries* (Issues and Information Series). The *iiSeries* currently offers fifteen books, and you'll find them here: https://store.dseusa.org/collections/books/down-syndrome-issues-and-information.

Pre-Primer through Grade School

There is a broad spectrum of reading readiness and skills among children with Down syndrome and other developmental disabilities in this wide age bracket. Because of this, I'm treating resources for pre-primer through grade school as one level, since some eighth graders may be reading at a pre-primer level.

Special Reads Books and Bundles

In this category, I include my reading program, *Special Reads for Special Needs* (http://www.specialreads.com), with bundles for Pre-Primer, Primer, and First Grade. The advantage of this program is that is has unusually high appeal for children and combines "heart and brain." Each level contains humorous picture books on the topic of favorite kid foods; that's for the heart—to hook the learner's interest. The actual design of the books is for the brain: a high-focus format, with large type, double spacing between all words, separation of text and illustration—all brain-friendly components that I've detailed in this book.

Each glossy picture book has its own interactive CD designed by a speech-language pathologist. The CDs contain literacy and language activities, as well as PDFs of printable flash cards.

Bundles come in three levels: Pre-Primer, Primer, and First Grade. Each bundle includes glossy picture books, interactive CDs, and printable CDs containing picture books that teach the essential high-frequency word lists, along with printable flash cards. Here is a sample of contents from the first level, the Pre-Primer Bundle

High Frequency Word Picture Books

An essential component of teaching reading is to help the child acquire a solid knowledge of high-frequency words. Those words are typically abstract and meaningless to children who are focused on the fun things of life. The "Dick and Jane" series in the United States and the "Peter and Jane" series in the United Kingdom did a good job of repetitively drilling these words years ago, but the illustrations and storylines don't hold the interest of today's children.

I was unable to find a book series to take the place of those books. My search led me through series of books that were so padded with more advanced reading lists that they were useless to my students with developmental delays. Eventually that led to my development of a series of seven books that incrementally teach those essential-but-boring words to our learners, from the Pre-Primer, Primer, and First Grade Dolch word lists. Those books are on *Special Reads Printable Discs* and can be either printed with their flash cards or read on screen (www.specialreads.com >Books & Bundles >Reading Bundles).

For some of my students with either visual problems or focusing issues, I teach these high-frequency books on screen as a first choice (pdf format); that helps both vision and attention for these students.

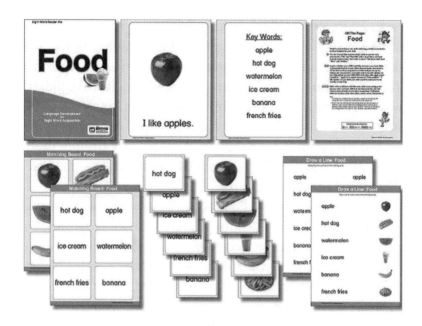

Lotto Games: Down Syndrome Foundation of Orange County

As I have mentioned, I have not yet found commercially available lotto games that use large type and place the words in a different order than the pictures on the respective boards. But here is the next best thing to making lotto games yourself: http://www.dsfoc.org/learning-program-store. There you can buy several dozen thematically organized reading kits on topics such as "Pets," "Feelings," and "At the Beach." The kits include picture- and word-matching boards and flash cards on the given theme that can be used to play lotto (as well as a book and worksheets). Here is a sample of one of the individual sets, "Food." Published by the Down Syndrome Foundation of Orange County, these sets are reasonably priced and give you plenty of material to work with. You'll need to make your own large red-letter flash cards to actually *teach* the words to the student "Sandwich style" before and after playing the game.

3. Other Published Materials That May Work Well

Enter: apps that are designed for typically developing children but can also teach children with developmental delays quite well. The number of apps now published is legion and growing exponentially. A quick walk through Apple's app store will give you more options than you could ever use. Pay attention to the reviews from parents and educators, and on top of their recommendations, use my brain friendly filter: look for apps that are

1. clear

2. uncluttered

3. designed using as large a font as you can find, and

4. able to be customized, if possible

New programs and apps are being designed on a continuing basis, so it's a good idea to keep your Internet search current to find new materials that can engage your learner.

Always look for the clear way into your student's perceptions. Yes, you can hopefully engage and entertain along the way, but when you're choosing teaching apps, make sure that you're maximizing the brain's chance of receiving and retaining the information.

Letter Sounds

The app I prefer for teaching letter sounds is *Starfall ABC*. I've mentioned this app earlier, but it is important to repeat it here. The website (www.starfall.com) is excellent for many reasons, but I favor the app for teaching letter sounds. That's because when it is teacher-controlled, by a simple repeated tapping of the letter, the educator can request that the child repeat the sound again and again before moving on to another letter sound. The sounds are clear, so this app can double as an excellent tool for teaching articulation as well as letter sounds.

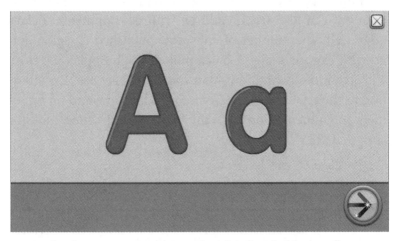

It also has entertainment value for the children in between their work of reproducing the letter sounds they hear. If you have a choice of using apps on either a smartphone or a tablet, do choose the tablet because of the larger visuals.

Working Memory Games

What is working memory? It's an executive function skill. Imagine you're working in front of a real desk, not a computer. Working memory is your desk. Imagine that I put a number of objects on your desk and ask you to sort them, sequence them, etc. Because they're at your desk, you can see them all and manipulate them. That is what working memory function is like: it holds information temporarily in your brain so you can work with it. Working memory involves concentration and is absolutely key to learning.

There are two types of working memory: auditory and visual-spatial. Children with Down syndrome are typically weak in the former and strong in the latter. Memory games can increase the strength of a child's visual-spatial working memory.

Any app that engages a child in playing memory games is helpful; it is not necessary for the game to contain words. Images stimulate working memory well and hold the learner's attention. You can help to develop working memory by using a variety of memory games, since each game will offer new and different elements. Again, size is important, so use a tablet computer when possible, rather than a smartphone. Look for the same hallmarks that you look for in any app or any materials: clarity, large size of pictures/type, and uncluttered layout.

The simplest way to play the memory game I described in chapter 6 is with a picture card collection. Lakeshore Learning Company (www.lakeshorelearning.com) has an excellent collection of picture cards divided by categories. To find it, search on Lakeshore's site for "Building Language Photo Library." The only drawback to this or any similar photo collection is that the reverse side typically has the word printed on it—or worse, another photo entirely. We want the card to be blank on the reverse side so the child has no tips as to the card content; she has to use her memory. In teaching, I've used opaque white tape to cover the words on the reverse side of this set from Lakeshore Learning, with no problem:

To see how a simple memory game can be played with our students, you can watch this video: https://www.youtube.com/watch?v=Uso_Q2B8N4k.

CHAPTER

15

Scaffold for Teaching, Step by Step

1. **Read aloud from birth.**

   a. Cultivate a love of language, books, and reading in the child by reading aloud two or three times a day—naptime, bedtime, anytime! Choose the best of children's literature for this. You are *not* teaching reading with this activity; you are awakening a love of books, stories, and reading. You are also modeling language and grammar. Reading aloud rocks!

   b. You can start actually *teaching* reading when the child can match picture-to-picture and has a receptive language of fifty-plus words (meaning that the child can understand, not speak, at least fifty words).

2. **Teach letter sounds and shapes first.**

   a. Use *Starfall ABC* and other apps to teach both letter sounds and shapes. Though the letter names are sounded in the Starfall app, the letter sound can be stressed by repeatedly tapping the letter. That feature makes this app ideal for teaching letter sounds.

   b. If you like, you can use Montessori sandpaper letters to help the child trace a letter with a finger (find these online). Or use *Handwriting Without Tears* and similar materials or apps for tracing shapes (www.hwtears.com).

c. Any *clear, uncluttered, large-type* app can be used to teach letter sounds as long as it uses the brain-friendly elements I've stressed in this book. Don't waste your time and risk student disengagement with apps that don't use these elements.

3. **Introduce letter names next.**

a. In addition to using brain-friendly apps, you can use the Fast Flash method to teach letters and numbers, using letters-only and numbers-only cards. These can be difficult to find, but any flash cards that show only a letter (no picture) or a number (no picture) are ideal. Search on Amazon for ready-made cards. If you're interested in free downloadable cards, try these two resources:

   i. For both lowercase and uppercase, try www.eslflashcards.com. Here is a direct link to the page you want: http://tinyurl.com/gwyzxj7.

   ii. Look for "lowercase alphabet flashcards," "uppercase alphabet flashcards," and " simple numbers 1–20 flashcards" at www.supersimplelearning.com.

b. Use the traditional ABC song because memorization is easier for the brain when coupled with music.

4. **Commit to teaching five minutes twice a day to begin with.**

a. Decide on this commitment and know for certain that frequency and consistency will pay big dividends in the end.

b. Remember that there are only two teaching options for accomplishing this goal of skilled, independent reading:

    i. "pedal to the metal," which works

    ii. "start and stop," which doesn't

c. Have the goal of working yourself out of a job through this commitment!

d. Increase the length of teaching time gradually as the child experiences success and gains confidence and enthusiasm.

e. Try to stop each session just before your learner is ready to stop.

f. Choose a teaching time when your child is not hungry, tired, or in a bad mood!

5. **Remind yourself of your teaching goals.** Your goals are:

a. to teach the child to *read for meaning, read for content;*

b. to help the child learn to love books;

c. to teach the child to seek books for high-quality entertainment, and later on, for information;

d. to make reading so attractive and successful that reading can compete successfully with electronic devices and entertainment.

6. **Limit the amount of time a learner spends on electronic devices for entertainment.** Remember:

a. Research indicates that learning and retention of information is more effective from a printed page than a screen.

b. Neurological changes take place with extended screen time, and those changes are not helpful to learning! If you're interested, read the book *iBrain* by Gary Small, MD, and Gigi Vorgan.

    c. Devices are not babysitters; they are rewards for cooperating, learning to behave appropriately, etc.

7. **Follow the same teaching routine each time, if possible.**

    a. Prepare the child to learn through cross-crawl exercise, Super Brain Yoga, or other "Brain Gym" exercises. Using a child-specific "ritual" at the start of each teaching session primes the learner and is always a great idea.

    b. Position yourself for teaching across from the child; ideally, you want to be no more than two feet away. This puts flash cards about twelve inches from the student's eyes when you flash them, which is ideal. We don't teach flash cards from a distance!

    c. Both learner and teacher use pointers to follow along in books, etc.

    d. Eliminate as many distractions as you can: visual, auditory, etc.

    e. Use low incandescent light; avoid fluorescent lighting. For a student who is easily distracted or agitated, you can use a flashlight pen for fun, focus, and "ownership."

8. **Memorize the brain-friendly design** for all materials.

    a. Use only high-interest material at first.

    b. Use large font size (32 pt. to 150 pt. or larger).

    c. Double-space or even triple-space between *all* words.

    d. Insert extra space between lines.

    e. Use sans serif fonts only.

f. Include lots of white space surrounding the text.

g. Use "text-alone" pages at the beginning of the learning process; no competing pictures on the visual plane for an emergent reader.

h. Put "pictures with text" pages after each text-alone page in the early stages of learning (see chapter 4 on personal books). You can also follow a text-alone page with a picture-alone page; this works as well, with the picture describing what the text said on the previous page. We don't give a picture cue before we show the text! We are teaching real reading, not guessing or reference.

i. Transition eventually to books that show text-with-pictures as the reader advances and gains fluency.

9. **Create "high-interest personal books"** and their **flash cards.**

a. Teach high-*interest* words derived from personal books as a first step.

b. Introduce first vocabulary from these personal books or personal lotto games (family matching games, etc.).

c. Create flash cards to teach the vocabulary in the personal books.

d. Using personal books, teach high-*frequency* words in their natural flow as connectors, seemingly almost incidental to the child. Remember that high-*frequency* words are never the primary focus of learning to read, contrary to the approach you might be facing in the classroom. The primary focus for the child will be the high-*interest* words used in his personal books.

10. **Use the Fast Flash technique for teaching sight words.**

   a. Use large cards (for emergent readers, the smallest size you want to use is 5" x 8" index cards).

   b. Use large type (32 pt. to 150 pt. or more, depending on the reader's age).

   c. Present the cards in groups of five words.

   d. Include a minimum of three high-interest words in a group when possible.

   e. Name and flash one or two cards *per second.*

   f. The child *does not say* the word but only focuses on the cards. You are the only one naming the word when you use this technique. If you're flashing the cards at the correct speed, there should not be time for the student to repeat the words.

   g. Do three repetitions of each group, one right after the other. Don't do more repetitions at that time, or you'll encourage boredom.

   h. Add additional groups of five cards, as the child is receptive and ready.

   i. Remove learned cards and replace with new ones.

11. **Create high-interest lotto/matching games.**

   a. Design high-interest picture boards and word boards with a field of four to six to a board (family members, friends, pets, favorite foods, etc.).

   b. Use these boards and their corresponding cards showing a field of two, three, four, or six by covering part of the board for beginners.

   c. Create large red-letter flash cards for each word; teach Sandwich Style, Fast Flashing the cards both before and after playing the lotto game.

d. Follow the graduated steps of difficulty from picture to picture, through to the most difficult level: matching pictures to words. (Review chapter 14 for a list of the seven steps of difficulty.)

e. These are especially useful testing tools for readers who are nonverbal.

12. **Develop phonemic awareness, decoding ability.**

a. Begin with CVC words (consonant-vowel-consonant), those words with three letters. Work first on beginning sounds, then on ending sounds, and finally on middle sounds.

b. Use apps, phonics games, and phonics-based toys for practice.

c. Use *Starfall ABC* and other apps for teaching sounds.

d. Try the decoding technique in *Teach Your Child to Read in 100 Easy Lessons* by Siegfried Engelmann et al.

e. Use phonics techniques suggested in *Teaching Reading to Children with Down Syndrome* by Patricia Oelwein.

f. Use phonics techniques suggested in *Try Reading Again* by DeAnna Horstmeier.

13. **Use the Sandwich Style teaching method.**

a. Fast Flash the words (three repetitions) in groups of five cards.

b. Read the book/materials aloud with the student. (As the student learns the vocabulary, the teacher's reading gradually drops out.)

c. Fast Flash the words again (three repetitions).

14. **Introduce picture books designed to teach high-*frequency* words.**

a. Use Fast Flash to teach the high-*frequency* words just as you use it to teach high-*interest* words.
b. To keep the learner engaged, make groups of five cards by mixing both high-interest and high-frequency words together in each group of five cards.
c. Use Sandwich Style teaching.
d. Stay true to the brain-friendly format if you are creating these books yourself or searching for ready-made ones.
e. High-frequency books can be found in the *Special Reads for Special Needs* printable series for Emergent, Primer, and First Grade levels at www.specialreads.com.
f. Gradually help the learner to progress through the seven sequential books in the *Special Reads for Special Needs* high-frequency series, through to second-grade reading readiness.

15. **Introduce modified trade books.**

a. Introduce these early, at the same stage as personal books, if you like.
b. Use for students of all ages to engage interest in reading; these are especially valuable as learning tools for more advanced readers and for older emergent readers. If you take the time to modify high-interest trade books for older nonreaders, those books serve the same purpose as what we used to call "hi-lo books," books designed for readers with higher age interests but low reading level. These, plus personal books, can make all the difference in the world for launching a teen or adult who is not yet reading.
c. Always choose high-interest trade books that are age appropriate.

d. Follow brain-friendly format guidelines (see chapter 5, "Designing for the Brain" or, in this chapter, look again at #8 in this list.)

e. Create flash cards for all of the most important words.

f. Use Fast Flash to teach the important words first. Later you can expand and create flash cards for more words, but begin with cards for just the most important words (character names, important action verbs, etc.).

g. Teach Sandwich Style: Fast Flash a group (or groups) of cards three times—read the book—Fast Flash three times.

16. **Blend strategies and materials for diversity and success.**

a. Like shuffling a deck of cards, mix together personal books, high-frequency word books, modified trade books, flash cards, and phonics, comprehension, and fluency work.

b. Keep diversity and freshness in your teaching; this gives you the best possible chance to keep your learner engaged.

c. Rely on your intuition to choose what will best keep the student interested and progressing.

d. Avoid learner boredom with the use of high-interest, diverse materials and diverse methods as well.

17. **Prioritize reading for meaning as a direct line to comprehension.**

a. Emphasize *reading for content* as a consistent goal to increase long-term comprehension skills.

b. Do not interrupt the child with corrections; keep a running record of errors and then do decoding work with those errors later.

c. Use "sticky notes" to aid comprehension and discussion and to implement sequencing.

d. Try color-coding Q & A in a text as a helpful first step to teaching the learner to refer to the text for answers.

e. Provide the student with ongoing assistance with comprehension questions that require making inferences, which is much more challenging.

18. **Foster fluency with these tips.**

a. Have the student read a sentence, paragraph, etc., three times in a row.

b. After reading aloud two times, have the learner read silently a third time.

c. Alternatively, read *with* the child during the third reading; this can give him early experiences with fluency and speed.

d. Don't interrupt the child with corrections; do decoding work later based on your running record of errors.

e. Use the "Magic Pull Card" (chapter 11).

f. Give quick verbal prompts that don't interrupt the flow.

g. Have the student read aloud daily; fluency comes from practice.

19. **Use errorless testing techniques.**

a. Use *matching* first: have the student match identical word cards by sight.

b. Use *selection* next: say a word aloud and have the student select the correct word card from a field of two, three, four, etc.

c. Use *naming* last: present the student with word cards to name (to read aloud).

d. Use this order of testing to avoid "Fear of Failure" syndrome and to keep the student successful and encouraged.

20. **Consider one-on-one pullouts for teaching reading in the classroom.**

a. Whether to have child stay in the classroom to learn reading or go with one-on-one pullouts for reading is an individual choice. But if your learner has Down syndrome, it's good to use the DSEI's research as a guideline, which shows measurable improvement when pullouts are practiced. See http://tinyurl.com/zftnwge for the research article.

16

The Backstory

Who Knew?

In 1990 in a tiny library in Northern Michigan, my son Jonathan's life changed and mine along with it.

I was staring dumbfounded at the new librarian who had just asked me the most unexpected question. "Can he read?" He gestured toward five-year-old-Jonathan-who-clearly-had-Down-syndrome. When I recovered, I politely replied, "No." Inwardly, I was thinking, "They'll teach him that in school, won't they? When he's older, maybe eight years old?" How little I knew about the low expectations awaiting him in a 1990 classroom!

"He could read *today* if you knew how to teach him," the librarian said.

I wonder if educator Greg Czarnecki, as he turned out to be, had any idea that he had just altered the course of my life with that conceptual earthquake. "Spend five minutes with me, and I'll show you how," he continued.

Needless to say, I later spent far more than five minutes with this father of a globally delayed teenage daughter. Greg had spent several years working with Glenn Doman's Institutes for the Achievement of Human Potential (IAHP). As he explained, though some aspects of IAHP's labor-intensive approach were controversial, "the gem of the IAHP is the reading program. If Jonathan enters kindergarten reading, the school system's expectations of him will skyrocket." He was, as it turned out, absolutely correct in that prediction.

By that time, I was a published author and a graphic designer/illustrator, so my skills meshed very neatly with those needed to create books that would make my son soar as a reader. My many years (since age thirteen) teaching children various skills, coupled with Greg's instruction, further study and research, and my professional background, paved the way for Jonathan to become an independent reader by age eight. His triple diagnosis of Down syndrome, attention deficit hyperactivity disorder (ADHD), and oppositional defiant disorder (ODD) was, in the end, no obstacle to his becoming an excellent reader.

His last official reading assessment was in early high school; he tested as reading at a seventh-grade reading level. Comprehension lagged behind at a fourth-grade level—a lag which we expect and with which I was quite satisfied: newspapers are standardly written at a fourth-grade level.

The only time I ever regretted his reading ability was possibly when he was in middle school and totally bored during a physical ed class. He idly looked at a red box on the wall that said, "Emergency. Pull down."

"Sure," he thought. "I can do that." And he did.

The school, by law, had to empty itself of all students and staff while the fire trucks obligingly roared into the schoolyard.

Jonathan spent the rest of the day suffering extreme boredom on a chair in the principal's office. Aside from that incident and his many requests for books and music that he finds on his online searches, we're good.

Whether he is reading his subscription magazines, his books (his collections include fairy tales, Bible stories, coffee-table Disney documentary books, and more), or his new Broadway musical programs (he saves every single program); scouring eBay and Amazon for books and CDs (correctly spelling their titles in the search boxes); or telling me I'm going the *"Wrong way!"* on the highway, the ability to read has transformed Jonathan's life. It is my passion and hope that it will do the same for your learner, regardless of age, interests, or "assessed" ability.

References and Resources

Articles

American Speech-Language-Hearing Association. "Definition and Symptoms of CAS/Childhood Apraxia of Speech." http://www.asha.org/public/speech/disorders/ChildhoodApraxia.htm.

Marshal, Lisa. "Medicine, Family Shape Fran Hickey's Journey." (Diagnostic overshadowing of autism & Down syndrome.) *CU Medicine Today* (October 2011). http://www.ucdenver.edu/academics/colleges/medicalschool/administration/alumni/CUMedToday/profiles/Pages/Fran-Hickey.aspx.

Books

Anderson, Ole. *Learn with the Classics: Using Music to Study Smart at Any Age.* San Francisco: LIND Institute, 1999.

Buckley, Sue, and Gillian Bird. *Reading and Writing for Individuals with Down Syndrome,* Down Syndrome Issues and Information series. Hampshire, United Kingdom: The Down Syndrome Educational Trust, 2001.

Campbell, Don. *The Mozart Effect: Tapping the Power of Music to Heal the Body, Strengthen the Mind, and Unlock the Creative Spirit.* New York: Harper Collins, 2001.

Dennison, Paul. *Brain Gym and Me: Reclaiming the Pleasure of Learning.* Ventura, CA: Edu-Kinesthetics, 2006.

Doman, Glenn, Janet Doman, and Douglas Doman. *How to Teach Your Baby to Read.* The Gentle Revolution series. New Hyde Park, NY: Square One Pub., 2006.

Engelmann, Siegfried, Phyllis Haddox, and Elaine Bruner. *Teach Your Child to Read in 100 Easy Lessons.* New York: Simon & Schuster, 1983.

Froehlke, Margaret, and Janet Zaborek. *When Down Syndrome and Autism Intersect: A Guide to DS-ASD for Parents and Professionals.* Bethesda, MD: Woodbine House, 2013.

Hale, Natalie. *Down Syndrome Parenting 101: Must-Have Advice for Making Your Life Easier.* Bethesda, MD: Woodbine House, 2012.

Harvey, Stephanie, and Anne Goudvis. *Strategies That Work: Teaching Comprehension for Understanding and Engagement.* 2nd ed. Portland, Maine: Stenhouse Publishers, 2007.

Horstmeier, DeAnna. *Try Reading Again: How to Motivate and Teach Older Beginners, Age 10 and Up.* Bethesda, MD: Woodbine House, 2012.

Oelwein, Patricia Logan. *Teaching Reading to Children with Down Syndrome: A Guide for Parents and Teachers.* Bethesda, MD: Woodbine House, 1995.

Facebook Pages

Hale, Natalie. *Down Syndrome Reading with Natalie Hale.*
Ulmer, Christopher. *Special Books by Special Kids.*

Organizations

Down Syndrome Education International
+44 (0)300 330 0750 (United Kingdom)
info@dseinternational.org
https://www.dseinternational.org/en-us

Down Syndrome Education USA
info@dseusa.org
https://www.dseusa.org/en-us

Down Syndrome Foundation of Orange County
info@dsfoc.org
http://www.dsfoc.org

Handwriting Without Tears
301-263-2700; 301-263-2707 (fax)

info@hwtears.com
http://www.hwtears.com/hwt

Institutes for the Achievement of Human Potential (IAHP)
215-233-2050
institutes@iahp.org
https://iahp.org

National Association for Child Development (NACD)
801-621-8606
www.nacd.org

Reading Materials Resources

Lakeshore Learning. lakeshore@lakeshorelearning.com.www.lakeshorelearning.com.

Love and Learning. www.loveandlearning.com.

Mrs. Perkins's Dolch Words. www.mrsperkins.com.

Right Brain Education. www.rightbraineducationlibrary.com.

Special Reads for Special Needs. www.specialreads.com.

"Step into Reading" series (Random House). www.stepintoreading.com.

YouTube

"Brain Gym Exercise for Students." 2013. https://www.youtube.com/watch?v=O5ChXC-rHLE.

Burns, Martha. "The New Brain Science of Learning" (TEDxEnola). 2012. https://www.youtube.com/watch?v=ahSYwchh-QM.

Dehaene, Stanislas. "How the Brain Learns to Read." 2013. https://www.youtube.com/watch?v=25GI3-kiLdo.

"Extraordinary Women, Episode 13: Maria Montessori" (documentary). BBC. 2014. https://www.youtube.com/watch?v=1Kuv0766wz8.

"John David Does His ABCs." 2016. https://www.youtube.com/watch?v=i3HIpEtwUKU.

"Michael Rosen on Phonics," BBC. 2007. https://www.youtube.com/watch?v=M4uocSjKcIQ.

Natalie Hale. 2016. (Down Syndrome Teaching Videos for Reading).

https://www.youtube.com/user/DownSyndromeReading.

"Super Brain Yoga." 2008. https://www.youtube.com/watch?v=KSwhpF9iJSs.

Index

About the Author

Natalie Hale is an award-winning author, an innovative educator, a parent of an adult son with Down syndrome, and for over two decades, a national and international speaker on the topic of teaching reading to learners with Down syndrome and other developmental delays.

In 2000, she founded *Special Reads for Special Needs* to provide parents and educators with reading books and materials specifically designed for learners with special needs (www.specialreads.com). Her Facebook page, Down Syndrome Reading with Natalie Hale, is a popular source of teaching information.

Her previous books with Woodbine House are *Down Syndrome Parenting 101: Must-Have Advice for Making Your Life Easier,* winner of Best Special Needs Parenting Book 2012 About.com Reader's Choice Award, and *Managing My Money: Banking and Budgeting Basics*, a finalist in the USA "Best Books 2011" Awards. She is also the author of the book, *Oh, Brother! Growing Up with a Special Needs Sibling*.

Natalie currently lives in Los Angeles and tutors reading through the Down Syndrome Association of Los Angeles. She continues to travel and teach parents and educators across the country and across borders through her reading workshops.